The Servant of Two Masters

Carlo Goldoni

Adapted by David Turner
and Paul Lapworth

D0710789

Samuel French — London
New York - Sydney - Toronto - Hollywood

© 1973 BY DAVID TURNER AND PAUL LAPWORTH

Rights of Performance by Amateurs are controlled by Samuel French Ltd, 52 Fitzroy Street, London W1P 6JR, and they, or their authorized agents, issue licences to amateurs on payment of a fee. **It is an infringement of the Copyright to give any performance or public reading of the play before the fee has been paid and the licence issued.**
The Royalty Fee indicated below is subject to contract and subject to variation at the sole discretion of Samuel French Ltd.

> Basic fee for each and every
> performance by amateurs   Code M
> in the British Isles

The Professional Rights in this play are controlled by The Agency (London) Ltd, 24 Pottery Lane, Holland Park, London W11

The publication of this play does not imply that it is necessarily available for performance by amateurs or professionals, either in the British Isles or Overseas. Amateurs and professionals considering a production are strongly advised in their own interests to apply to the appropriate agents for consent before starting rehearsals or booking a theatre or hall.

ISBN 0 573 11412 9

Please see page iv for further copyright information

THE SERVANT OF TWO MASTERS

This play was first presented at the Queen's Theatre in London by Michael Codron on 18th December 1968. The cast was as follows:

DOCTOR LOMBARDI, a lawyer	Ken Wynne
BRIGHELLA, an innkeeper	Ronald Radd
SILVIO, son of LOMBARDI	Clive Francis
PANTALONE, a rich merchant	Graham Crowden
SMERALDINA, CLARICE's maid	Michele Dotrice
CLARICE, daughter of PANTALONE	Morag Hood
TRUFFALDINO, a servant	Tommy Steele
BEATRICE RASPONI, of Turin	Julia Lockwood
FLORINDO ARETUSI, of Turin	Edward de Souza
FIRST PORTER	John Rapley
SECOND PORTER	Bunny May
OLD WAITER	John Crocker
YOUNG WAITER	Kenneth Shanley
SERVANTS	Hazel McKay
	Amanda Duckett
MUSICIANS	Peter Honri
	Tony Reiss
	Adrian Harman
Directed by	Toby Robertson
Scenery and costumes by	Alan Barrett
Music by	Ben Pearce Higgins
Lighting by	Tony Corbett

COPYRIGHT INFORMATION

(See also page ii)

This play is fully protected under the Copyright Laws of the British Commonwealth of Nations, the United States of America and all countries of the Berne and Universal Copyright Conventions.

All rights including Stage, Motion Picture, Radio, Television, Public Reading, and Translation into Foreign Languages, are strictly reserved.

No part of this publication may lawfully be reproduced in ANY form or by any means — photocopying, typescript, recording (including video-recording), manuscript, electronic, mechanical, or otherwise—or be transmitted or stored in a retrieval system, without prior permission.

Licences for amateur performances are issued subject to the understanding that it shall be made clear in all advertising matter that the audience will witness an amateur performance; that the names of the authors of the plays shall be included on all programmes; and that the integrity of the authors' work will be preserved.

The Royalty Fee is subject to contract and subject to variation at the sole discretion of Samuel French Ltd.

In Theatres or Halls seating Four Hundred or more the fee will be subject to negotiation.

In Territories Overseas the fee quoted above may not apply. A fee will be quoted on application to our local authorized agent, or if there is no such agent, on application to Samuel French Ltd, London.

VIDEO-RECORDING OF AMATEUR PRODUCTIONS

Please note that the copyright laws governing video-recording are extremely complex and that it should not be assumed that any play may be video-recorded for whatever purpose without first obtaining the permission of the appropriate agents. The fact that a play is published by Samuel French Ltd does not indicate that video rights are available or that Samuel French Ltd controls such rights.

INTRODUCTION

There is no one way of performing **The Servant of Two Masters,** and the production described in this version underlines the point. The play provides a theatrical vehicle adaptable to the skills and abilities of varied companies of actors. It has a knockabout style, uninhibited in its high spirits, but necessitating a carefully controlled production from both actors and stage staff. The play also offers a rich range of characterisation and a subtle analysis of social attitudes both between men and women and between different classes. These elements in the play and the opportunities open to a producer are best understood against the background of the commedia dell'arte tradition.

Mid-eighteenth century Italy had seen a decline in its improvised drama, the commedia dell'arte, primarily owing to a dearth of actors skilled in the genre. The players were abandoning their masks, and learning their dialogue by heart. Two important dramatists reacted very differently to this state of affairs. The aristocratic Carlo Gozzi (1720-1806) sought to defend and preserve the traditional commedia dell'arte; the bourgeois Carlo Goldoni (1707-1793) accepted the decline of the commedia and tried to develop a new drama out of the old form.

The essence of commedia dell'arte is that the play before production consists of a scenario and on this framework the actors generate the dialogue themselves. In its use of a stock collection of plots and masks it clearly has an ancestry in a very much more ancient comedy. The atmosphere of improvisation does not bring out a rough-and-ready attitude to performance in the actors; it demands definition and polish. Commedia dell'arte was the Comedy of the Accomplished Artist, the arte part of the label indicating both professional skill and the existence of professional companies, the essence of the style being found in the group-playing of troupes who worked together over a long period. These companies of players graduated from the squares of great Italian cities such as Venice, Bologna and Florence to the sophisticated courts of European kings and princes.

The plot-line of the comedy within which the actors improvised their dialogue had foundations in a collection of stock-types, and these characters have become as famous as any theatrical convention in existence: Harlequin, Columbine, Pantalone and Pierrot. The art of this comedy is seen in the work of famous dramatists like Molière, and its traditions created a vigorous progeny seen in pantomime, Punch and Judy shows, the mimes of Marcel Marceau, the 'pierrots' of park and pier, and the comedy of Charlie Chaplin. The term 'slapstick' goes back to the commedia dell'arte, the 'slapstick' being the bat used by Punch, Harlequin and Scapin to beat other characters, perhaps to gain a laugh when the jokes of the improvised dialogue were failing. Several painters down the centuries have been fascinated by the characters of the commedia dell'arte, notably Watteau, Tiepolo and Picasso.

The modern pantomime still shares with the old commedia dell'arte the possibility of endless variations within the old established story. Much of the continuity and humour depended upon the lazzi or bits of comic business such as acrobatics, water-tricks or other horse-play.

The standard collection of characters gained variety by drawing on regional Italy for its types and dialects, such as Tuscan, Paduan and Venetian. The dramas were thereby firmly rooted in the affections and interests of Italian audiences and the travelling companies would make a feature of the regional type appropriate to the setting of the performance. The place of origin could have a temperamental significance or an occupational reference. Pantalone, the miser, traditionally comes from Venice, city of merchants and bankers; the Doctor, filled with pedantry, naturally comes from the ancient university city of Bologna; while Bergamo, home of Harlequin, was supposed to be the home of slow-witted people.

Although the general pattern of characterisation was fixed, these types nevertheless developed and changed and sometimes a puzzling detail proves to be a surviving trait from an earlier tradition of the character.

Pantalone was normally an ancient, greedy, talkative, avaricious, eminent and, usually, retired citizen of Venice. He dressed in red shirt, breeches, full stockings, Turkish slippers, black coat with flowing sleeves and soft fez-like cap. He would have a hooked nose and a long grey beard and he spoke in Venetian dialect, full of aphorisms. Violent in temper but peace-loving when violence threatens, it was Pantalone's fate to be duped. Towards the end of the seventeenth century, the character underwent a fundamental change, becoming a respectable head of family, anxious for his children, keen to keep his word of honour and with a respect for discipline. Mean and duped he might still be, but he became in essence a redoubtable bourgeois citizen. In Molière's plays we meet Pantalone in the characters of Orgon and Harpagon.

The Doctor, traditionally surnamed Lombardi, always hailed from Bologna, spicing his language with learned phrases and homilies. He was often consoled in friendship by Pantalone of Venice, and it became usual for him to be father of one of the lovers. His traditional costume was sober black dress and doctor's cap, white collar and cuffs. His dignity of manner, though heightened by speech interspersed with Latin phrases, often concealed his hypocrisy.

The most interesting commedia dell'arte character was Harlequin, usually the most adept at performing the lazzi. Dressed in a suit with patches sewn on, small hat, heel-less shoes and a black mask, he was traditionally full of acrobatics, falls, somersaults and dancing. One of several examples of Harlequin's theatrical progeny was the crafty, boastful valet who became in the eighteenth century a Bergamask comedian called Truffaldino, and was acted by one of the great performers of his day, Sacchi, who interpreted the role for both Gozzi and Goldoni between the years 1740-1770. Gozzi, of course, maintained that Truffaldino must remain an improvisation and that a script would be the death of the character.

Paired with Harlequin as a second Bergamask valet-buffoon, Brighella represented the cleverness of those people born high up on the hill in Bergamo, in contrast to the dim-wits of those born on the lower reaches, typified by Harlequin in some versions. Brighella is usually seen as the Intriguer, and early examples of the type were cynical, sharp and menacing, even murderous. The Brighellas of the eighteenth century commedia dell'arte are all pallid versions of the earlier villains, having developed into something much more in the nature of lackeys, their traditional yellow and black stripes still being part of many contemporary hotel servants' dress in the colouring of the waistcoats.

The prime element in the various pairs and quartets of lovers in the commedia dell'arte is their complete fatuity. Their intrigues of love are fated to become complex by virtue of the interventions of cranky old fathers and comic servants and their names are Flavio, Ottavio, Silvio, Orazio, Federigo, Lavinia, Lucinda, Clarice and Columbine. There are usually four lovers, either courtly or pastoral in background.

Gozzi and Goldoni

The use of masks gave permanency and a grand scale to all these established characters, but it also demanded a subtle expressiveness in the body-acting of the players. The group style and interdependence of the actors ensured the right emphasis and prominence of a role at any one moment and traditional styles of language and gesture added force to the playing. But it was the mask which constituted the main bone of contention between Gozzi and Goldoni, the former supporting its retention as being in the nature of the drama, while the latter rejected it as an obstruction to the actor's proper portrayal of subtle emotion. Their conflict focused on a second element - the dialogue. The masks limited the actor's scope in the development of a realistic characterization; improvised dialogue worked in the opposite direction, encouraging the actor to develop an individual interpretation in his performance. Goldoni's view looks towards the commonly accepted modern division of theatrical responsibility; the dramatist controls the content, the actor controls the performance.

The years 1740-60 saw the best of Goldoni in Venice. After that, subjected to the successful counter-attack of Gozzi, he left for Paris. Eighteenth century Italy gave the victory to Gozzi; the history of drama honours Goldoni.

The Servant of Two Masters as Commedia dell'Arte

Goldoni's play may be a piece of written dialogue without masks, but it also presents a recognisable exercise in commedia dell'arte. Goldoni's Pantalone, for example, presents us with the typical Venetian father, harassed by coping with a wayward daughter, mildly miserly, readily moved one way or another. But he also shows specific elements of other Pantalones. Scene 22 admirably demonstrates the avarice and snobbery of the character. Pantalone prefers to marry his daughter to the 'quality' represented by the Rasponis, and his determination to honour the contract with Rasponi similarly reflects the businessman's code of honour seen in the original commedia dell'arte merchant of Venice. An even more ancient version of the character, an old, toothless Pantalone is suggested by Brighella's jibe in Act II Scene 17, 'Pick a bone, sir? With your teeth?' and the meanness seen in the opening of the play, 'We don't want lavishness, do we?' and his hope that the visitor will not prove to be a relative who will drink him out of house and home.

Goldoni's Brighella is an eighteenth century version in his subdued devilry, but his ready agreement to keep Beatrice's secret at their first meeting in the play reflects his commedia dell'arte character combining roguishness and intrigue. This role developed quite naturally into that of the calm, observing psychologist.

Finally, Truffaldino embodies the tradition in so many ways. The duality of the character is stressed, as in Pantalone's description of him, either 'A rogue or an idiot'. Other characters express puzzlement in contemplating the possible truth of the character, saying he is one thing or the other, but avoiding acceptance of one interpretation to the exclusion of the other. This mixed nature, shrewdness or idiocy, is demonstrated in Scene 31. Other traditional elements in the role were the cockiness, the stupidity, and his incipient but frustrated gluttony. Truffaldino loves style in life, nevertheless, as may be seen in his concern for the manner of the food's presentation in the great scene of serving two masters at table. There is a kind of rebellion in him, too: the servant on whom they depend, but a servant who will let them down by taking them literally.

In the original Italian play by Goldoni, we find Smeraldina saying she likes 'the swarthy or dark-faced little fellow'. The sentiment was retained for the London production featuring Tommy Steele, but not the description, for obvious reasons. The original line indicates a reference to the black-faced or black-masked Harlequin ancestry of Truffaldino.

Goldoni's Innovations

Goldoni's innovations are more interesting than his debts to the commedia dell'arte. As Goldoni was Venetian, bourgeois, and trained in the law, people displaying one or more of these characteristics are treated in kindly fashion. Indeed, Goldoni shows a gentler manner than his master, Molière, and created a bourgeois comedy of ordinary people bewildered by the pressures of convention and class. Much depends upon the portrayal of the finer shades of relationships between classes - Pantalone higher than Brighella but lower than Beatrice, richer but less cultured than the Lombardis. Venice was a republic, but its elected doge and hereditary nobles gave it an aristocracy Goldoni considered worthy of satire, and he turned a mocking gaze upon many aspects of aristocratic pretensions. Florindo, typically named, has to be an elegant gentleman of the period, slightly dandy and 'silly ass', possessing a Tuscan ascent, the equivalent of a twentieth century Oxford voice. Goldoni clearly enjoyed the mildly ridiculous and substituted jollity and good humour for the original coarseness of much of the commedia dell'arte. Coarse indecencies seem to have been part and parcel of the commedia improvisation, and in the process of converting the scenario into a written script it lost most of its theatrical vulgarity and became more realistic.

Goldoni's most famous innovation was his creation of spirited heroines to replace the more modest and demure young ladies called Adriana, Isabella and Laura. He looked upon women as individuals and not merely as the subordinates of men. In Beatrice we see a Goldoni woman, replacing the anonymous heroines of the earlier tradition, even more assertive and self-aware than Shakespeare's Rosalind and Viola. Beatrice seeks liberation, a hand in her own destiny, and obviously delights in the disguises and machinations that arise from her self-determined ambition. Brighella appreciates her boldness and proclaim: her 'rare spirit'. In Act I Scene 5 she says, 'I'll not be bothered with any of them. I want freedom.' Clarice refuses to accept her father's choice of husband and, in the second act, Smeraldina, the servant girl, speaks out for women's rights too. In Act II Scene 8 she attacks the old difference of double standards: 'Women have the reputation of being unfaithful, while you men commit infidelities.' She says more on the subject in Act II Scene 16, admitting that despite the unfairness of the position between the sexes, the biological pressure wins in the end: 'man wants woman, woman wants man. You're bound to get married some time or other.' Despite her lower social rank, Smeraldina proves to be as bright, witty and self-possessed as her 'betters'. Beatrice may be the prime example of the liberated woman, and Clarice may follow her a close second in choosing her mate against her father's wishes, but it is Smeraldina who sounds the clarion call to modern woman in Scene 27 when she defends Clarice: 'If woman made the laws, things'd be different.'

Thus, Goldoni took the orthodox commedia dell'arte and turned it into a written comedy despite the objections of his more successful rival, Count Carlo Gozzi. The abandonment of improvisation and masks made the comedy more realistic and in content and theme Goldoni was notably sympathetic towards the bourgeoisie and to women.

Goldoni's Achievement

Many critics of European drama underrate Goldoni's achievement. He lacks irony, sharpness of satire and profundity, but as a theatrical craftsman in the comic genre he is brilliant. The Servant of Two Masters has all the Goldoni virtues of comic set-pieces, hilarious scenes of farce and a rapidly moving plot. In addition, it has Truffaldino.

Goldoni's greatest art consists in exploiting the potential of the comic
complication only to the point that it avoided repetition. Having made
the best of a comic situation, Goldoni does not repeat his effect; he
moves on to the next inevitable complexity. He has an instinctive feeling
for the correct length of each scene as it exploits and then advances the
action. The length and patterns of the scene are extremely variable.
Some scenes are ritualised, measured and formal; others through
duologues provoke confrontations and conflict; then he will create solo
declarations, revelations prevented, and all the tricks of theatrical
fun of which Truffaldino's tour de force in waiting on two tables is the
best example. A large number of scenes encompass this splendid
variety, although in effect there are only three locations. The scenes
vary in length and tone, and there is need for variation in pace. Goldoni
successfully exploits the changes in mood and these are further brought
out in the language varieties created by Goldoni: The cool dignity of
Beatrice, the rough, bluff assurance of Pantalone, the foolish
extravagance of Silvio and Clarice, the foppishness of Florindo and the
pompous learning of Doctor Lombardi.

THE LONDON PRODUCTION

Setting

A single multi-purpose set was used in the London production, with
plenty of entrances R. and L. and a sweeping staircase and archway
up-stage. A well R. and a table L. completed the basic set, and the
use of curtains helped to convert an exterior into an interior set. A
basic location was suggested R. as Pantalone's house while the L.
roughly represented Brighella's Inn. A simplified version of the set
might have three entrances on both R. and L. sides with the addition of
the archway entrance U.S.

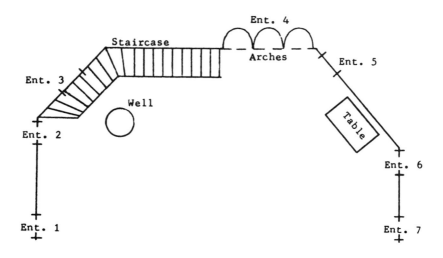

Production Points

The 1968 London production was performed with one interval. In the
Italian version Act Two began at this translation's Scene 22 when the
humiliated Silvio seeks satisfaction from Pantalone.

In the London production Tommy Steele maintained commedia dell'arte
traditions by incorporating set-pieces of business. At the end of Act
One Scene 6 when Truffaldino bemoans his humdrum servant's life, a
mimed sequence over a tango rhythm was inserted, displaying a
'lion-tamer joke' in which Tommy Steele put a row of imaginary lions
through their circus paces. Similarly, Truffaldino's operatic duet with
himself, his exit with the pudding, and the general street scene in Act
One, all present the equivalents of commedia dell'arte lazzi. These
non-essential pieces are indicated in the text as 'inserts'. The play
does demand, however, a great deal of essential comic business as may
be observed in the great serving scene and in the mixing of the clothes
from the trunks. It is in the nature of the play for both obligatory
business and the 'inserts' to be a matter of the producer's taste and
imagination. Producers and companies may contrive business and
set-pieces to suit their own talents. The 'inserts' and many of the
invented effects may be omitted.

Character of Truffaldino

The character is carefully established and used for different comic effects as the action develops. Truffaldino has a joy in the attempted tour de force, the exceptional, the playful, the unexpected challenge. He is always hungry, seeking food despite the obstacles of service. Yet he is no respecter of persons; he serves without servility. When he cringes before a beating, he realistically seeks to assuage his punishment. Truth is relative to him. His service partly consists of trying to tell people what they want to hear.

There are five linked elements in Truffaldino's contribution to the action, and these are concerned with character, motif and situation:

(1) **Hunger motif:** Truffaldion's obsession with his belly, with food and his know-how in matters of table.

(2) **Twin aspects of the character:** throughout the play, other characters are puzzled by Truffaldino's character, and offer contrary interpretations. It adds up to an acceptable ambiguity in our view of him.

(3) **The Great Fixer Image:** this is Truffaldino's own view of himself. He delights in the challenge of circumstances, even intensifying the difficulties Fate throws up to him and he boasts quite openly to the audience.

(4) **Endearing Idiot image:** in his courtship of Smeraldina he is ridiculous but attractive and in his illiteracy and inspired folly similarly he makes us laugh on his side. Only his and Smeraldina's mutual betrayal run counter to this view, but this exemplifies the natural sense of self-preservation found in their class at the time.

(5) **Comic Discomfort:** this is the prime theatrical purpose of the role. The mixture of Great Fixer and Endearing Idiot contribute to place Truffaldino in a sequence of demanding situations.

Music

Goldoni's play does not require music. A musical element, however, was a feature of the London production and indications of its use have been retained in the text. Music was used to suggest the sunny, Italian atmosphere, to indicate changes of mood and to support pieces of business. A specially produced tape of original music was augmented on-stage by live musicians; the latter are not essential to the achievement of the musical effects noted above. It would be difficult to find eighteenth century music capable of providing the excitement expected by a modern audience. Consequently, if music is used to heighten the dramatic effect it is better to think of such well-known styles or pieces as may reflect the appropriate moods. Opera, Neapolitan love-songs, and twentieth century café music could all be used, such material being readily available on LP records. The use of music may be much more restricted than this version of the play suggests, or it may be omitted completely.

DAVID TURNER and PAUL LAPWORTH

THE SERVANT OF TWO MASTERS

ACT ONE

Scene One

Music. A room in PANTALONE's house. PANTALONE, DOCTOR LOMBARDI, SILVIO, BRIGHELLA, SMERALDINA standing in frozen positions on stage. Lights come up and, as music fades, they move.

DOCTOR	(turning to PANTALONE) Signor Pantalone, we are met here for the happy occasion of the betrothal of my dear son, Silvio.
PANTALONE	We are, Doctor.
DOCTOR	Then bid your daughter come forth, sir, <u>et ergo accidat</u>.
PANTALONE	Smeraldina. Fetch your mistress.
	MUSIC
SMERALDINA	(bobs) Sir.
	(SMERALDINA exits. MUSIC continues as CLARICE enters followed by SMERALDINA.)
ALL	Ah.
	(While CLARICE comes gracefully in, the DOCTOR speaks to his son.)

DOCTOR	To her, my son. Give her your hand.
SILVIO	(moves to CLARICE) Clarice, here is my hand - and with it, take my heart.
PANTALONE	Well, go on, daughter. Don't be shy. Simple ceremony and you're engaged.
CLARICE	Silvio, here is my hand. I promise to be your wife.
SILVIO	And I to be your ever loving husband.
ALL	Ah.
DOCTOR & OTHERS	Bravo! Excellent!
DOCTOR	Brighella, you will swear you have borne witness to this.
	(SERVANT enters with a tray - jug of wine and two glasses. PANTALONE takes them and gives the smaller glass to the DOCTOR, keeping the bigger one for himself. CLARICE and SILVIO kiss.)
BRIGHELLA	I will indeed, sir. I hereby witness the betrothal between your dear son Silvio and the lovely lady Clarice, and if I may say so, sir, I don't think there had better be a very long engagement.
PANTALONE DOCTOR	(together) Clarice! Silvio!
	(The lovers break apart.)
PANTALONE	I respect your sentiments, my dear Brighella. I've no desire for there to be a long engagement this time.
DOCTOR	This time? What is that you say? This time?
PANTALONE	Ah, well, there's something a little delicate, something that we never quite got round to speaking about. I think this is the proper time to tell him, Clarice, don't you?
CLARICE	Silvio knows already.

PANTALONE   And you're quite happy about it?

SILVIO   Why, of course, sir.

DOCTOR   What is it then? What is it?

PANTALONE   Sorry, well, it's simply this. My daughter Clarice has been engaged before.

DOCTOR   What?

PANTALONE   Don't worry. She never saw the feller. It was all done by proxy, you understand?

DOCTOR   I see. But then, hasn't this fellow a claim to her?

PANTALONE   No. You see the poor chap's gone to a better place. Passed over.

DOCTOR   Dead?

PANTALONE   Yes, he had the call - and he went.

DOCTOR   I see. And who was this gentleman?

PANTALONE   A certain Signor Federigo Rasponi of Turin.

DOCTOR   And what did he die of?

PANTALONE   Killed in a duel. They say it was because of his sister - to save her honour or something. Anyway he was struck down - fatal blow.

BRIGHELLA   It came as a very nasty shock to me, I can tell you, sir.

PANTALONE   You knew him?

BRIGHELLA   Oh yes. I was three years in Turin afore I settled here.

PANTALONE   Then you have the advantage of me, sir. I never clapped eyes on the fellow. Everything was done by letter.

BRIGHELLA   Yes, I knew him very well, and what's more, I knew his sister, too. A proper tomboy, she was - rode a horse like this. (Miming riding astride.) Not like this. (Miming side saddle. Laughs.) Ha, ha! A right lass. And the brother was proud of her - too proud to my mind. Would never let her marry. And now he's dead. Ah, well, we never know what fate has in store for us, do we, sir?

DOCTOR   No - no - no. The ways of the Lord are many and devious.

PANTALONE   So, Doctor, seeing that my dear daughter has never been within one hundred miles of her late fiancé, there can be no possible harm done, can there?

DOCTOR   I agree. A clear case of <u>corpore absente</u>, <u>virgo intacto</u>.

(Both raise their glasses to CLARICE, who curtsies.)

PANTALONE   Quite, eh? But let us not talk of madness. (He collects DOCTOR's glass and gives both to SERVANT, who goes out.)   My dear Brighella, the gentle doctor here is of my disposition. We decided against any guests or relations. We don't want lavishness, do we?   (To BRIGHELLA.)   So how about preparing us some tasty dish or other?

BRIGHELLA   My privilege and pleasure, sir. And you could do no better than to eat at my inn in the square over there, sir.

(They hear three loud knocks.)

PANTALONE   Someone knocks, Smeraldina, see who it is.

SMERALDINA   At once, sir.   (She goes out.)

PANTALONE   I only hope it's not a relative. They'll stay all day and drink every bottle in the cellar.

CLARICE   Father, with your permission -

PANTALONE   Yes, my dear?

CLARICE   If you have a visitor, Silvio and I would like -

(SMERALDINA returns.)

PANTALONE   (to CLARICE)   A moment, a moment.   (To SMERALDINA.)   Yes, what is it?

SMERALDINA   Sir, it's the servant of some stranger or other. He says nothing to me. He says he wants to give you a message.

PANTALONE   Let him come in. Let's hear what he wants.

(SMERALDINA leaves.)

Yes, my dear. You were saying?

CLARICE   If you have a visitor, Silvio and I would like to withdraw.

PANTALONE   What? Withdraw? Go off by yourselves? You'll stay here.

Scene Two

The same. TRUFFALDINO enters, followed later by SMERALDINA.

TRUFFALDINO   Greetings, respects and heartiest salutations to one and all.   (To audience.)   And I must say a very nice quality of person we've got here - very nice indeed.   (Looking at CLARICE.) Who's the lovely lady then? What are you doing tonight, sweetheart?

PANTALONE   How dare you, sir. That is my daughter.

TRUFFALDINO   Congratulations, sir. Well done.

PANTALONE   I beg your pardon.

SMERALDINA   Signora Clarice is engaged to be married.

TRUFFALDINO   Oh well, it's not my day, is it? And what might your role be in this menage, may I ask?

SMERALDINA   I'm Smeraldina, her maidservant.

TRUFFALDINO   Maidservant, eh? What are you doing tonight?

PANTALONE   Enough of that, sir. Leave her alone. Just tell
               me, who are you? What do you want and where
               do you come from?

TRUFFALDINO   Who? What? Where? Three questions all at
               once.   (He touches his head.)   It's too
               much for me.

PANTALONE   (aside to DOCTOR)   The man's a numbskull -
               a blockhead.

DOCTOR   (aside to PANTALONE)   A comical fellow to
               be sure.

PANTALONE   Now look here, sir. Who are you?

TRUFFALDINO   My name, sir, is Truffaldino. By trade, a
               servant - a humble servant to my master.
               (To SMERALDINA.)   What time do they let
               you out?

PANTALONE   Your master, sir? Your master? Who is he?

TRUFFALDINO   Why, he's the gentleman who is waiting outside to
               come in and pay you his respects.

PANTALONE   This gentleman, sir? What's his name?

TRUFFALDINO   His name? That's fair - straightforward. One
               question at a time. I'll answer that. He is none
               other than the right worthy Signor Federigo
               Rasponi of Turin.

ALL   What!

TRUFFALDINO   That went well!

PANTALONE   Come here, sirrah. That name. Say it again.
               I couldn't have heard you correctly.

TRUFFALDINO   (aside)   The poor old fellow's hard of hearing.
               (He yells into PANTALONE's ear.)   Signor
               Federigo Rasponi of Turin!

PANTALONE   (pushing his finger into his ear)   Get away!
What the -   (To DOCTOR.)   He's mad,
absolutely mad.   (To TRUFFALDINO.)
I'll have you know, sir, Federigo Rasponi of
Turin is dead.

TRUFFALDINO   Dead!

PANTALONE   Dead as a doornail.

TRUFFALDINO   My master - dead?

PANTALONE   Quite, quite dead.

DOCTOR   No shadow of doubt.

TRUFFALDINO   But I've only just left him outside. He was very
much alive then. Accident, was it?   (Suddenly
dawns on him.)   Just a moment! Dead, sir?
You've killed him.

PANTALONE   What?

TRUFFALDINO   While I had my back turned, talking to the lady
here, one of you slipped out and done him in.
Who was it?

DOCTOR   (approaching TRUFFALDINO)   Now look here -

TRUFFALDINO   Don't you come near me. I've heard all about
you city folks. You Medicis, you Borgias.
Vendetta, was it? Knifed him in the back while
I was being affable, did you? I must see it for
myself.   (He goes out.)

PANTALONE   Well, what do you make of that? What is he?
A rogue or an idiot?

DOCTOR   He's a bit of both, if you ask me.

BRIGHELLA   Rogue, no: idiot, yes.

SMERALDINA   No, simple and good, that's how I put it.
(To audience.)   I liked him.

PANTALONE   And what's all this about Signor Federigo?

CLARICE   Heaven help me, if it is true.

PANTALONE	We've letters, girl, telling us he's dead.
SILVIO	(to CLARICE) Even if he is alive, he'll have come far too late. (Taking her hand.) You are mine.
	(TRUFFALDINO returns.)
ALL	(startled) Aha!
TRUFFALDINO	Aha! Oh, gentlemen. You naughty pair. (Wagging his finger.) You naughty, naughty pair.
PANTALONE	(aside) He's raving – absolutely raving.
DOCTOR	(aside) Agreed.
TRUFFALDINO	Allow me to learn you your manners. Gentlemen what are proper gentlemen have respect for servants. They don't go playing around with them.
PANTALONE	We must be careful – he might be dangerous. What's the matter, sir, the world's been treating you badly, has it?
TRUFFALDINO	Did you or did you not tell me that Signor Federigo was dead?
PANTALONE	What of it?
TRUFFALDINO	He's still very much alive, thank you very much. Still waiting outside in the street to come in and pay you his respects.
PANTALONE	Signor Federigo?
TRUFFALDINO	Signor Federigo.
PANTALONE	Rasponi?
TRUFFALDINO	Rasponi.
PANTALONE	Of Turin?
TRUFFALDINO	Of Turin.
PANTALONE	Ha. Those who are mad ought to go into hospital.
TRUFFALDINO	Now look, sir, before I resort to bad language

I'll put it to you again: if you go outside in the street you'll see him - Signor Federigo Rasponi waiting on the corner. And if you tell me once more he's dead, I shall be forced to use a certain word.

PANTALONE (lifting his hand)   You are asking for a beating, sirrah!

DOCTOR Calm, Signor Pantalone, calm. Tell him to ask this so-called Signor Rasponi to come in.

TRUFFALDINO At last! In future, gentlemen, I trust you'll know how to handle men of quality, honourable fellows from Bergamo like myself.   (To SMERALDINA.)   Young lady, we'll talk again! I go!   (He goes out upstairs.)

CLARICE (quietly)   Silvio, I tremble with fear.

SILVIO (quietly)   Whatever happens, you're mine.

DOCTOR Now let the truth be revealed.

PANTALONE 'Tis some cock and bull story to swindle me.

BRIGHELLA Rely on me, sir. I'm the only one here who's ever seen Signor Federigo. I'll soon tell you if it's him.

SMERALDINA (to audience)   He's not a liar, that servant; he's as good as gold. I can sum up men, don't you worry, and I know when they're nice. (To PANTALONE.)   Sir, by your leave. (She goes.)

Scene Three

The same. BEATRICE enters in man's dress.

BEATRICE	Signor Pantalone?
PANTALONE	Sir?
BEATRICE	Allow me to issue a rebuke.
PANTALONE	Eh?
BEATRICE	I send my servant to you with a message and you keep me standing in the street for a whole half hour.
PANTALONE	Excuse me, sir, but truly who are you?
BEATRICE	I am Federigo Rasponi of Turin.
PANTALONE	You are Federigo Rasponi of Turin!
	(ALL show astonishment.)
BRIGHELLA	(aside) What's all this about? This isn't Federigo; it's his sister, Beatrice. What's she up to, I wonder?
BEATRICE	You have heard, no doubt, that I am dead?
PANTALONE	That sums it up, yes.
BEATRICE	Killed in a duel?
PANTALONE	Exactly.
BEATRICE	Thanks be to heaven, I was only wounded.
PANTALONE	Wounded!
BEATRICE	And I am come here to Venice to claim the money you owe me.
PANTALONE	(clutching at the DOCTOR) Oh, no-no, no-no, no-no, no.
	(SMERALDINA enters U. L. and takes BEATRICE's hat, stick and gloves and exits U. L.)

DOCTOR

Calm now, Signor Pantalone, calm!
(Moving to BEATRICE.)   Tell me, Signor,
have you authority, recommendation, testimonial,
signature, stamp or stigmata about you, to prove
to us your identity?

BEATRICE

Your doubts are just. Here are four letters
from business correspondents, people Signor
Pantalone knows well.   (Gives DOCTOR four
letters.)   You will recognise the handwriting
and assure yourselves of who I am.

(BRIGHELLA coughs loudly. BEATRICE sees
BRIGHELLA and her face drops. She makes a
mute 'ah'. Aside.)

Brighella here. He recognises me. Should he
reveal who I am, I am lost. I must forestall
him.   (Aloud to BRIGHELLA.)   Friend,
you seem to know me.

BRIGHELLA

That I do. I believe you know me too. Brighella
Cavicchio's the name.

BEATRICE

(moves to BRIGHELLA)   Yes, I remember
you well. Tell me, what are you doing here in
Venice?   (Aside.)   Do not give me away.

BRIGHELLA

(aside)   Have no fear.   (Then aloud.)
Why, sir, I run the inn in the square over there.
I am ever at your service.

BEATRICE

Splendid. In that case, I shall be staying there.

BRIGHELLA

Honoured guest you'll be, sir.

(BEATRICE turns and walks to PANTALONE.)

(Aside.)   What's her game then?

BEATRICE

(to PANTALONE)   Satisfied, signor?

PANTALONE

I've examined them -   (He blinks weakly.)
Er - yes -

BEATRICE

As a further proof. Signor Brighella knows me
and will vouch for who I am.

BRIGHELLA	That I do, rest assured.
BEATRICE	What is my name?
BRIGHELLA	Your name?
BEATRICE	The truth, sir.
BRIGHELLA	Rasponi!
BEATRICE	You hear? I am Federigo Rasponi of Turin.
CLARICE	No. He can't be.
BEATRICE	Tell me, sir, who is this young lady?
PANTALONE	Why, sir, this is Clarice, my daughter. (Aside.) Now for some fun!
BEATRICE	Clarice? Then she is the one who is promised to me in marriage?
PANTALONE	Just so, sir, just so.
SILVIO	No, sir. Never, sir, never.
BEATRICE	Pray, sir, who are you?
SILVIO	Signora Clarice, sir, is betrothed to me.
BEATRICE	To you?
SILVIO	Yes, sir, she's mine.
BEATRICE	How dare you, sir! You are speaking of my promised bride.
CLARICE	(rushing to PANTALONE and gripping him) Oh, father.
PANTALONE	There now, Clarice, there. Dear Signor Federigo, I must reveal all. I truly believed that you were - er - how shall I put it?
BEATRICE	Dead?
PANTALONE	That's the word. So I offered my daughter to Signor Silvio here, and at the very last moment you have turned up. But there's no damage done. You have got the prior claim, sir. There you are! Clarice is yours.

CLARICE	What?
BEATRICE	Come, Clarice, come to the arms of one who adores you!
SILVIO	Stop!
BEATRICE	Eh?
SILVIO	Do you think, sir, that I would ever allow that? You might be Federigo Rasponi, but I am Silvio Lombardi.
DOCTOR	Well said, my son! Long live the Lombardis!
SILVIO	Exactly! Now should Signor Pantalone here do me this wrong, why then I shall have my revenge. Whosoever tries to take my Clarice from me must first face me with the sword and then, sir, we shall fight to the death. Clarice, sir, is mine.
	(SILVIO leaves. The DOCTOR follows him and calls after him.)
DOCTOR	I'm proud of you, my son. Proud. (To the rest.) Long live the Lombardis! (He hurries after his son.)
BEATRICE	Dearest lady bride, all this must be very distressing for you.
CLARICE	Don't come near me. Why can't you go back to where you came from?
BEATRICE	But we have signed a contract - we are bound to each other for life.
CLARICE	Oh, father! Must I marry him?
PANTALONE	That you must.
CLARICE	Oh!
PANTALONE	So dry your eyes, and try to make yourself presentable.
CLARICE	Oh!
PANTALONE	Go to your room.

CLARICE	Oh!
PANTALONE	Obey your father.
CLARICE	Oh!
PANTALONE	Go.
CLARICE	Oh! No! (She leaves, weeping.)

Scene Four

The same.

BEATRICE	Signor Pantalone, we must do all we can to treat her gently. In truth, sir, I pity the girl.
PANTALONE	So do I, sir, so do I. But I am a man of business. I've made a contract - contracts must be honoured.
BEATRICE	Exactly, sir.
BRIGHELLA	Well now, if you're going to stay at my inn, I'd better go and make the necessary arrangements. So you're going to marry Signora Clarice, are you? That will be nice!
BEATRICE	That is enough, my man.
BRIGHELLA	(going up steps) Excuse me! (To PANTALONE.) Your servant, sir. (He goes out.)
BEATRICE	And now, sir, to business. Shall we examine our accounts?

PANTALONE	(crosses to bell and rings it) Yes, let us do so. They are in order. I shall have them delivered to your room at the inn, shall I?
BEATRICE	If I am not about, give them to my servant, will you?
PANTALONE	Your servant?
BEATRICE	Don't worry. He is thoroughly reliable. You can trust him with anything.

(A SERVANT enters with BEATRICE's hat, stick and gloves, hands them to her and then goes out.)

PANTALONE	Very well, then, I'll do as you say. I shall see you soon - son-in-law.
BEATRICE	At your service, dear father.

(Music starts as they both go out.)

* Insert No. 1   General entrance to music. Boy wheeling ice-cream cart enters calling 'Ices - ices - get your lovely ices!' SMERALDINA enters with straw mat and carpet beater. She beats mat. Serving-girl with empty shopping basket enters, crosses and beckons three musicians to enter, playing as they come. Girl then goes out. TRUFFALDINO enters and grabs an ice-cream off cart. Boy grabs it back and wheels cart out, followed by the musicians. TRUFFALDINO acknowledges SMERALDINA who goes out with mat and beater. Old waiter enters and dusts table. TRUFFALDINO mimes short conversation and goes out. Old waiter goes out. * BRIGHELLA, wearing hat, enters and then sits laughing. BEATRICE enters with hat and stick and crosses BRIGHELLA, not seeing him. Music fades.

Scene Five

Street before Inn. BRIGHELLA sees BEATRICE.

BRIGHELLA	(laughing) Oh, madam, you really fooled them, didn't you?
BEATRICE	(turning) Shhh!
BRIGHELLA	You do like your little practical jokes, don't you?
BEATRICE	This is no joke, this is something serious.
BRIGHELLA	(rising) Oh?
BEATRICE	(taking BRIGHELLA aside) Do you know who killed my brother, Federigo?
BRIGHELLA	Well, I heard tell it was Florindo Aretusi.
BEATRICE	Florindo, my lover.
BRIGHELLA	Yes, madam.
BEATRICE	His family told me that he had fled here to Venice, so I decided on the instant that I would follow him. I took my brother Federigo's clothes to support my disguise and his letters of credit.
BRIGHELLA	Here, you're not going to trick Signor Pantalone out of his money, are you?
BEATRICE	Trick? The money is mine. My brother dead, I am his heir.
BRIGHELLA	Then why not tell him the truth?
BEATRICE	Think, Brighella, think. Should I tell him that I want the money to help Florindo? Why, they would try to hasten me to either an asylum or a nunnery. I'll not be bothered with any of them. I want freedom.
BRIGHELLA	Truly, madam, you've a rare spirit.
BEATRICE	Then help me, Brighella, please.

BRIGHELLA   Trust me, I'll help you.   (He kisses her hand.)
Oh, that manservant of yours –

BEATRICE   What about him?

BRIGHELLA   He seems a bit of a blockhead to me.

BEATRICE   Maybe – but he is loyal. To me loyalty is
everything.

BRIGHELLA   True, very true. This way – sir!

                   (BEATRICE goes out, followed by BRIGHELLA.)

Scene Six

The same. TRUFFALDINO enters.

TRUFFALDINO   I'm right fed up, I am. I do nothing but hang
around all day long, doing nothing. I wouldn't
mind but I'm starving hungry, too. Ever since
I met this master of mine on the road from
Turin, not a morsel has passed these lips. I'm
so hungry I feel quite faint. Mind you, it's
my own fault. I chose the wrong master. He
never eats, my one. Have you noticed, he's got
no stomach on him to speak of. It's all – plenty
of that.   (He mimes walk with stomach
tucked in.)   You should always choose a
master with plenty of –   (He mimes a big
stomach.)   Mind you, there's masters and
masters, you know. There's them as got
respect for servants, give them a decent place
to sleep, decent food, but my one – he's not in
the place five minutes and he's off, visiting and

leaving me hanging about. Well, I'm hungry,
I'm fed up and I'm broke, and it's rotten being a
servant. I'm going to change my job. I want
something more exciting - something out of the
humdrum.

* Insert No. 2 I'd like to be a lion-tamer. And what's wrong
with that? (He snarls.) That's a lion.
(He snarls again.) Another lion.

(Music. He cracks imaginary whip and goes into
mime of lion-tamer's act. He ushers in
imaginary lions and positions them. He counts
them and one is missing. He goes over to well
and listens and then lifts lid. One jumps out.
TRUFFALDINO slams down lid and hits lion's
paw, who limps and whines. He positions a
lion C. and strokes its head. He rolls up his
sleeves and starts to open lion's mouth. He gets
his head into lion's mouth, grimaces and takes
head out with expression of disgust.) *

But what can I do? I'll have to be a servant.
I'm not trained up for anything else.

(Music. TRUFFALDINO crosses and leans
against wall.)

Scene Seven

The same. FLORINDO ARETUSI is seen strolling along the back. He
wears a top hat and carries a sword-stick. He is talking over the
music as he comes.

FLORINDO (off) Thank you, gondolier. Come along,
porter, it must be along here, and turn right.

	(As he enters.) Ah, here we are, Villa Brighella. Come along, come along.
	(PORTER enters. He is bent double under a large trunk and carries a wicker basket and a long carpet bag with a butterfly net sticking through the handles.)
PORTER	Ugh - ugh - ugh - the weight's killing me. (He drops the lot.)
FLORINDO	Careful, man, careful.
PORTER	(sits on trunk exhausted) No good, I'm done for.
FLORINDO	But the inn's only just over there. It's only two or three steps. Pick it up, pick it up.
PORTER	Sorry, it's me for the knacker's yard. Ruined.
TRUFFALDINO	(aside) This looks like my chance to earn a halfpenny or two.
	(Music fades.)
	Can I be of any assistance, sir?
FLORINDO	Ah, yes. I'm trying to get my things into this inn.
TRUFFALDINO	Say no more, sir. Leave it to me. Always a privilege and always a pleasure, sir. (He moves to the PORTER who is still seated on the trunk.) Get off.
PORTER	Eh? Who are you?
TRUFFALDINO	You heard. Get off.
PORTER	Oh, I can't get up. He's done me an injury, he has.
TRUFFALDINO	Hard luck. (He pulls the trunk from under the PORTER who falls to the ground. TRUFFALDINO picks everything up and heads towards the inn.) Won't be a moment, sir. (Enters the inn.)

FLORINDO	Good man. (Then to PORTER who has picked himself up.) What are you waiting for?
PORTER	Your token of appreciation, sir.
FLORINDO	You know, that's what I thought you might be doing. There you are and good luck to you. (Gives him coins.)
PORTER	Thank you, sir. Very civil of you. (Looking at coins.) What's this? Three ha'pence. Ruddy top-hatted stinker. (He goes out.)

Scene Eight

The same. TRUFFALDINO returns.

TRUFFALDINO	I have taken the liberty of booking you in, sir.
FLORINDO	Good man.
TRUFFALDINO	A very nice room you've got, sir, very superior. I've also done a tour of the kitchens: lovely food and very big helpings. Oh, yes, highly recommended, sir.
FLORINDO	Now, look here. What's your name?
TRUFFALDINO	Truffaldino Battachio de Bergamo Vecchio, sir.
FLORINDO	Well now, Truffaldino, may I ask what you do?
TRUFFALDINO	Do, sir?
FLORINDO	For a living.
TRUFFALDINO	Me, sir? I'm a servant, sir.
FLORINDO	Are you working for any one at the present

	moment?
TRUFFALDINO	At the present moment, I am working for no one at all.
FLORINDO	So you are without a master, then?
TRUFFALDINO	I am as you see me, sir, without a master. (Aside.) Well, the other fellow's not here, so I tell no lies.
FLORINDO	Would you care to serve me?
TRUFFALDINO	Serve you, sir? Why not? (Aside.) If the pay's better, I'll swop. (To FLORINDO.) May I enquire, what would be my rerumination, sir?
FLORINDO	Your what?
TRUFFALDINO	My rerumination, sir?
FLORINDO	Oh, I see, your wages. (Laughs.)
TRUFFALDINO	Yes, sir.
FLORINDO	Well now, what would you expect?
TRUFFALDINO	Well, my other master gave me a pound a month and all found.
FLORINDO	Good. I'll do the same.
TRUFFALDINO	If you didn't mind, sir. I did feel I ought to better myself.
FLORINDO	Well. (Taking snuff.)
TRUFFALDINO	Shall we say a penny a day for snuff?
FLORINDO	Agreed.
	(FLORINDO offers TRUFFALDINO pinch of snuff. TRUFFALDINO takes it and FLORINDO puts remainder back in snuff-box.)
TRUFFALDINO	Thank you, sir. I'm yours, sir.
FLORINDO	Now then, Truffaldino, this is the first thing I'd like you to do.

TRUFFALDINO   I'm all ears, sir.

FLORINDO   I'd like you to go down to the post office -

(TRUFFALDINO gives colossal sneeze. FLORINDO looks at him coldly.)

Bless you. I'd like you to go down to the post office -

(TRUFFALDINO sneezes again.)

I'd like you to go down to the post office - (FLORINDO looks sharply at TRUFFALDINO who does not sneeze.)   and see if there are any letters for me. My name is Aretusi - Florindo Aretusi.

TRUFFALDINO   Florindo Aretusi. I've got it, sir.

FLORINDO   That's it. Good man. Now then, if there are any letters for me, I'd like you to bring them back to me here immediately.

TRUFFALDINO   You can rely on me, sir.

FLORINDO   I'm sure I can.

TRUFFALDINO   And in the meantime, would you consider ordering a small meal, sir.

FLORINDO   Yes, yes, I'll see to it. Off you go.

TRUFFALDINO   (going off)   Florindo Aretu -   (Huge sneeze.)

FLORINDO   Well, he's something of a joker perhaps, but nothing too displeasing. Do you know, I think I'll try him out for a day or two. Innkeeper, innkeeper!   (He goes off.)

Scene Nine

The same. TRUFFALDINO re-enters.

TRUFFALDINO	I thought I handled that very well. I told him my other master gave me a pound a week and all found. He didn't. He gave me a guinea. Well, whichever way you work it out, he's a better proposition than the other fellow. I mean, my other master was a bit soft round the gills, you know - a bit girlish. I would have had to have watched myself with that one. Oh well, I've a new master now, so off to the post office for him.
BEATRICE	(off) Truffaldino!
TRUFFALDINO	Ay, ay! It's the beardless wonder!

(Enter BEATRICE and BRIGHELLA.)

BEATRICE	Ah, Truffaldino, I'd like you to go this instant to the boat, take delivery of my trunk and bring it back to the inn.
TRUFFALDINO	Which inn?
BRIGHELLA	This inn.
TRUFFALDINO	(aghast, aside) I've got them both staying there now.
BEATRICE	Hurry along, man. Don't moon about.
TRUFFALDINO	Like lightning, sir.
BEATRICE	Ah! Just a moment.
TRUFFALDINO	Yes, sir.
BEATRICE	While you're about it, go to the post office and see if there are any letters for me.
TRUFFALDINO	At the gallop, sir.
BEATRICE	Hold it.
TRUFFALDINO	Yes, sir.
BEATRICE	You'd better ask if there are any letters for

Beatrice Rasponi as well.

TRUFFALDINO   Beatrice Rasponi. I take it the lady's your wife,
sir?

(BRIGHELLA laughs.)

BEATRICE   She is my sister.   (Nods to BRIGHELLA.)
She was to have come with me but at the last
moment she was indisposed.

TRUFFALDINO   Oh, I am sorry to hear that, sir.

BEATRICE   Certain friends of hers may have written to her,
so bring any letters there are, and I'll give them
to her when I return. Hurry along now, hurry
along.

(TRUFFALDINO goes out. BEATRICE re-enters
the inn. TRUFFALDINO comes back.
BRIGHELLA is by the table.)

TRUFFALDINO   (to audience)   Here, what with the shortage of
jobs -   (He sees BRIGHELLA and breaks off.)
'Ow do.

BRIGHELLA   'Ow do.

TRUFFALDINO   Are you the landlord here then?

BRIGHELLA   Yes, I am, and remember, if you want to eat
well, you had better behave well.

TRUFFALDINO   I was waiting to hear you say that.

BRIGHELLA   Right then. Off you go then.

TRUFFALDINO   I beg your pardon?

BRIGHELLA   I said, off you go.

(They both start to leave, and then turn.)

TRUFFALDINO
BRIGHELLA   (together)   Off you go!

(BRIGHELLA goes out.)

Scene Ten

The same.

TRUFFALDINO   (coming back)   There's enough people looking
                  for one master. I've got two now. Well, it
                  stands to reason I can't serve both of them, can
                  I? And why not? It'd be something, wouldn't it?
                  Two masters - double wages - double rations -
                  and If I was found out - double trouble. And what
                  if I was found out? If one of them sends me
                  packing, I can always stay with the other one.
                  When all's said and done, it's something to
                  boast of, isn't it? Something out of the humdrum.
                  Two masters, just like that   (He makes a
                  gesture of juggling.)   Right. I'm resolved.
                  I'm off to the post office for both of them.

                  (As he turns to go, SILVIO enters.)

SILVIO   (aside)   At last I have found the servant of
                  Signor Federigo Rasponi.   (To
                  TRUFFALDINO.)   Fetch me your master.

TRUFFALDINO   Which one?

SILVIO   Which one? What do you mean, which one?

TRUFFALDINO   I beg your pardon, sir. He's in the inn.

SILVIO   Then you fetch him.   (Pushing TRUFFALDINO
                  backwards.)   And tell him from me that if he
                  is a man of honour, which I doubt, he will come
                  forth immediately and meet me face to face.

TRUFFALDINO   Face to face?

SILVIO   Face to face. I hate him. So fetch him before
                  I break every bone in your miserable little body.

TRUFFALDINO   Oh well, it's a fifty-fifty chance. I'll send the
                  first one I find.

SILVIO   Don't dawdle, sirrah, or I'll beat you.

                  (TRUFFALDINO goes out.)

Scene Eleven

The same.

SILVIO	Ooo, I am resolved. Ooo, I am. Either Federigo here renounces all claims to my dear Clarice, or we shall put it to the test, life against life.
	(Enter FLORINDO and TRUFFALDINO.)
TRUFFALDINO	That's him, sir, only be very careful. He looks very dangerous to me.
FLORINDO	But I don't know him.
TRUFFALDINO	You don't know him.
FLORINDO	No.
TRUFFALDINO	Oh well, off to the post office. (He goes out.)
	(FLORINDO draws his sword-stick. SILVIO has already drawn his.)
FLORINDO	Sir.
SILVIO	Sir.
FLORINDO	You asked for me, sir.
SILVIO	I, sir?
FLORINDO	Yes, sir.
SILVIO	I beg your pardon, sir, but I do not know you, sir.
FLORINDO	But your servant told me that you threatened to issue a challenge.
SILVIO	He must have made a mistake, sir. I asked to see his master, sir.
FLORINDO	I am his master.
SILVIO	Are you?
FLORINDO	Certainly.

SILVIO	Oh. Do forgive me, sir, do forgive me. But your servant is the very image of a man I saw this morning.
FLORINDO	Eh?
SILVIO	His double, in fact. It's quite clear, sir, that I have made a terrible mistake, and I do crave your pardon, sir.
FLORINDO	You mean you mistook my servant for another?
SILVIO	Yes, well, I must have done, sir.
FLORINDO	(crossing to him and sheathing his sword) Ah well, there's no harm done. Mistakes often happen. (Laughs.)
SILVIO	(sheathing his sword) You are a stranger here, are you not?
FLORINDO	Yes, I am. I'm from Turin.
SILVIO	But the man I wish to speak to - he comes from Turin.
FLORINDO	Oh. Well, I'm sorry to hear it. Still, since he is a fellow countryman of mine, perhaps I can make peace between you.
SILVIO	Would you know a certain - Federigo Rasponi?
FLORINDO	Federigo Rasponi?
SILVIO	You know him?
FLORINDO	Well, I used to, only too well.
SILVIO	He intends to snatch from me - the woman I love.
FLORINDO	What's that?
SILVIO	My beloved - my betrothed. But I'll not let him, sir. No, I will kill him first.
FLORINDO	Kill him? But how can you kill him? He's dead.
SILVIO	Ah, yes, sir, so it was given out. But he gave us proof, he showed us letters.

FLORINDO   What! Not dead but -

SILVIO   No, sir. He lives.

FLORINDO   So - I did not kill him then.

SILVIO   He arrived in Venice this morning, sir, safe and sound.

FLORINDO   Federigo - here in Venice. I fly from justice and I come face to face with my enemy.

SILVIO   Sir, when you meet him, which you are bound to, as he is staying at this inn here -

FLORINDO   Here?

SILVIO   Yes, sir. I beg you to do me a tiny little service. Now, sir, when you see him, tell him, for his own good - (Half-draws sword.) you understand me, sir, for his own good - he must abandon all ideas of this marriage. (Sheathes sword again, brings heels together, and bows.) My name, sir, is Silvio Lombardi. You have my respect and my friendship.

FLORINDO   I am honoured, sir, and privileged, sir. (Aside.) And what is more, absolutely perplexed.

SILVIO   Would you grant me, sir, the favour of telling me your name?

FLORINDO   My name? Why yes, my name is - (Aside.) I must not reveal myself! My name is Grazio Ardenti, ever at your service.

SILVIO   Signor Grazio, I am yours to command.

FLORINDO   (clicking heels) Sir.

SILVIO   (clicking heels) Sir.

FLORINDO   Your servant ever.

SILVIO   Dispose of me as you will.

FLORINDO   (clicking heels) Sir.

SILVIO   Sir.   (Clicks heels too hard, hurts himself,
                        and limps out.)

                        Scene Twelve

The same. FLORINDO alone.

FLORINDO   What's this? Can the dead arise? Perchance I
                        did not touch a vital spot. I had not time to
                        watch him breathe his last. No, he lives.
                        Federigo Rasponi lives. What to do now? Ah,
                        my beloved Beatrice,

                        (Music.)

                        has he walled you up in a nunnery, then come
                        here seeking his revenge? Well, dead or alive,
                        what matter is he to me now? I'll to Turin -
                        back to my Beatrice. Immured as a nun - my
                        Beatrice - never!

                        (Music fades as FLORINDO goes out.)

Scene Thirteen

TRUFFALDINO enters with another PORTER who is carrying
BEATRICE's trunk on his back. The PORTER, bent under his load,
cannot see his way.

TRUFFALDINO	Straight on, mate. Hard right. Straight down. Left wheel.
FLORINDO	(off L.) Ah, Truffaldino!
TRUFFALDINO	Hold on. That's master number two, and this luggage belongs to master number one. What to do? Think! Got it. Into action. (To PORTER.) Back.
PORTER	Back?
TRUFFALDINO	Back, you fool. Into reverse.
PORTER	But I can't go back.
TRUFFALDINO	Keep going. Wait for me on the corner.
	(PORTER goes out the way he entered. FLORINDO enters.)
FLORINDO	Ah, Truffaldino.
TRUFFALDINO	Sir?
FLORINDO	I must leave for Turin. Will you come with me?
TRUFFALDINO	When?
FLORINDO	Now, immediately.
TRUFFALDINO	How about my dinner?
FLORINDO	Ah! First we eat, then we go.
TRUFFALDINO	In that case, a pleasure to accompany you, sir.
FLORINDO	Good man. Now, then, have you been to the post office?
TRUFFALDINO	I have, sir.
FLORINDO	Have you got any letters?

TRUFFALDINO	I have, sir.
FLORINDO	Give them to me.
TRUFFALDINO	Right, sir. (He takes three letters from his pocket and drops them. Aside.) Strike me! I've mixed them up. There's one letter for one master and two for the other, but which is which? I can't read.
FLORINDO	Come along, sirrah, give me the letters.
TRUFFALDINO	(marching up to him) A matter to report, sir.
FLORINDO	And what's that?
TRUFFALDINO	On the way to the post office I met a colleague, another servant. 'Going to the post office,' he said. 'Me,' I said. 'Yes,' I said. 'Save me a journey,' he said. 'See if there are any letters there for my master.' 'Anything to oblige an old chum,' I said. So there we are, sir. One of those letters isn't yours.
FLORINDO	(taking the letters) Ah well, that's all right, we'll soon get that sorted out. Let's see now. Florindo Aretusi. What? 'Beatrice Rasponi'. (Aside.) Beatrice. Here in Venice?
TRUFFALDINO	That must be the one for my colleague, sir.
FLORINDO	Who is this colleague of yours?
TRUFFALDINO	I've told you, another servant. Going under the name of – (He taps his forehead twice. The answer pops out of his mouth.) Pasquale.
FLORINDO	Pasquale?
TRUFFALDINO	Yes, sir, Pasquale.
FLORINDO	I see. And who is the master of this Pasquale?
TRUFFALDINO	Master, sir?
FLORINDO	Yes, what is his name?
TRUFFALDINO	I've no idea.

FLORINDO	No idea? But you must have some idea. When you went to collect the letters from the post office, you must have given a name.
TRUFFALDINO	Very well reasoned, sir.
FLORINDO	Well? What is it?
TRUFFALDINO	I've no idea.
FLORINDO	You've no idea?
TRUFFALDINO	My friend wrote it down on a piece of paper.
FLORINDO	A piece of paper? What did it say?
TRUFFALDINO	I'm sorry, sir, but I can't read.
FLORINDO	Well, where's the paper?
TRUFFALDINO	I left it with the man at the post office.
	(FLORINDO moves L., holding his brow.)
FLORINDO	Oh, my God.
	(TRUFFALDINO moves R. saying to the audience.)
TRUFFALDINO	(aside) I'm making it up as I go along.
FLORINDO	Now look here –
TRUFFALDINO	Yes, sir?
FLORINDO	This servant, this Pasquale.
TRUFFALDINO	Pasquale, sir?
FLORINDO	Where does he live?
TRUFFALDINO	I've no idea.
FLORINDO	No idea? Well, perhaps you'd be kind enough to tell me how you can give him back this letter?
TRUFFALDINO	That's a point.
	(Both laugh.)
FLORINDO	Well?
TRUFFALDINO	He told me to meet him on the town square.

FLORINDO	Did he?
TRUFFALDINO	Under the clock. Now, sir, if you'll give me the letter, I'll set about finding him.
FLORINDO	No. I shall open it.
TRUFFALDINO	What! But you can't read –
FLORINDO	Silence.
TRUFFALDINO	But it isn't –
FLORINDO	Silence! (He marches to the side of the stage tearing open the letter.) This letter is written to the woman I love. Beatrice and I are one. Shall I not read it then? Yes. 'Dear Lady, Your sudden departure from the town has caused much gossip. Everyone knows you have gone in search of Signor Florindo. The magistrates have found out that you are wearing men's clothing and have left nothing undone – (He looks up amazed – then turns letter over.) left nothing undone to trace you and make an arrest.' Oh, I see. (Laughs.) 'Take care, Madame, and Heaven bless you. I remain your humble and devoted servant, Maria della Doira.'
TRUFFALDINO	(to audience) No manners, you know, no manners! Fancy, reading other people's letters. He's a real nosey parker, that one.
FLORINDO	(aside) So – Beatrice has left home – wearing man's clothing – trying to follow my footsteps. Oh, my beloved – my dearest – how faithful – how devoted! Truffaldino!
TRUFFALDINO	Sir?
FLORINDO	Quickly. Go and find your Pasquale and ask him where his master lives. Bring me news of it. Away now.
TRUFFALDINO	The letter, please, sir.
FLORINDO	Oh, yes. There you are.

TRUFFALDINO	How am I going to explain its being opened, sir?
FLORINDO	Oh, don't worry about that.
TRUFFALDINO	(aside) Don't worry about that, he says.
FLORINDO	On your way. No time to be lost.
TRUFFALDINO	Still going to Turin, are we?
FLORINDO	Turin? No, certainly not.
TRUFFALDINO	Well, how about my dinner, then?
FLORINDO	I've got more important things to think about than your dinner. Go and find your Pasquale. (Aside.) Beatrice is here in Venice, so is Federigo; she must be found before she meets her brother. (To TRUFFALDINO.) Truffaldino, on your way - no time to be lost.
TRUFFALDINO	But, sir -
FLORINDO	Don't loiter about. Away with you. (He leaves.)

Scene Fourteen

The same.

TRUFFALDINO	What about that then? Still at least I'm glad he's not leaving. I'm anxious to see how I can manage my two servant jobs. I mean, it's a challenge to industry. If I pulled it off, I might get an award from the Doge. The problem is this letter. I can't very well deliver it open, can I? Well, first we fold it, then we seal it. It's not difficult if you've got a little knack. My

old granny once taught me how to seal letters
with chewed bread. How about that? Chewed
bread. The only problem is I haven't any bread.

(The YOUNG WAITER enters with a basket of
bread on his right shoulder. He crosses the
stage in front of TRUFFALDINO, whistling.)

'Ow do.

WAITER

'Ow do.

(As he crosses TRUFFALDINO mimes taking a
bit of bread from basket. Actually he has it in
his pocket. WAITER goes out.)

TRUFFALDINO

Well, we've got the bread. Extend the
forefinger and thumb of your right hand, take a
piece, place it in the oral position and chew.
(He does so.)   Oh, it's lovely.   (He panics.)
I've swallowed it.   (He takes another bite.)
Don't be a fool, Truffaldino. One last chance,
lad.   (He struggles with himself.)   It's
going - it's going - it's no good. Nature's
calling. Don't do it, Truff, don't do it.
(Business trying not to swallow bread.
TRUFFALDINO finishes kneeling, facing
audience - sticks out his tongue and the bread
chewed to a paste is on the tip.)   Paste!
I'm a great one for the household hint and the
practical tip.

(There is a loud whistle from the SECOND
PORTER off stage.)

PORTER

(off)   'Ere! 'Ow much longer I got to wait
then?

TRUFFALDINO

(sealing letter with the paste as he talks)   It's
the porter. I'd forgotten all about him. Straight
in here, mate.

(PORTER enters again with trunk on his back.)

Straight on.

(PORTER heads for the edge of the stage - just as he gets there:)

Hard left.

(PORTER wheels left.)

Scene Fifteen

The same. Enter BEATRICE.

BEATRICE	Ah, my trunk.
TRUFFALDINO	(to PORTER) Left again. Right on as far as you can go.
	(PORTER and trunk go out.)
BEATRICE	You got it here safely, then?
TRUFFALDINO	Everything's safe with me, sir.
BEATRICE	Have you been to the post office?
TRUFFALDINO	Yes, sir. And I've got a letter for your sister, sir.
BEATRICE	Ah, good. (She takes it.) This letter's been opened.
TRUFFALDINO	Opened, sir? Impossible, sir.
BEATRICE	Opened, and sealed up again, with - what is this?
TRUFFALDINO	Bread. I wonder how that came about?
BEATRICE	You don't know, eh? You good-for-nothing! Who opened it? Answer.

TRUFFALDINO	Kind sir, I crave your pardon. Allow me to confess the truth.
BEATRICE	What?
TRUFFALDINO	Er, when I got to the post office I found out there was actually a letter there for me too - from my dear old Granny. And as I can't read, I opened your letter instead of hers.
BEATRICE	If you can't read, why bother to open them at all?
TRUFFALDINO	I was anxious to feel the notepaper that Granny's loving hands had touched.
BEATRICE	In that case, I admire your sentiment.
TRUFFALDINO	So do I.
BEATRICE	(aside) Good kind Maria. What a faithful servant you are! (To TRUFFALDINO.) Well, my man, as my trunk has arrived, here is the key. (Gives him key.) Open it up and give my clothes an airing.
TRUFFALDINO	Certainly, sir. One key, one trunk.
	(BEATRICE goes out.)

Scene Sixteen

The same. FLORINDO enters just as BEATRICE leaves.

FLORINDO	Now then, my man, have you put my trunk in my room?
TRUFFALDINO	Yes, sir.
FLORINDO	Well, here is my key. (Gives

	TRUFFALDINO key.) Give my clothes an airing. Now then, what about this Pasquale?
TRUFFALDINO	Pasquale?
FLORINDO	Yes, Pasquale.
TRUFFALDINO	Pasquale who, sir?
FLORINDO	Your friend, the servant. You were to meet him in the town square, under the clock, and ask him whom he serves under. You remember?
TRUFFALDINO	Oh, Pasquale - the town square - under the clock. What's the time, sir?
FLORINDO	What's the time? (A clock chimes 'one' offstage.) It's one o'clock.
TRUFFALDINO	Well, there we are, sir. I'm not supposed to meet him till two-thirty.
FLORINDO	Not till then?
TRUFFALDINO	Two-thirty sharp. So that just about gives us time for a small meal, sir.
FLORINDO	What?
TRUFFALDINO	I believe it is customary around mid-day, sir.
FLORINDO	Yes. I suppose it is.
TRUFFALDINO	Well, if you'll kindly follow me this way, sir.
FLORINDO	What?
TRUFFALDINO	Order the food, sir.
FLORINDO	Oh, yes, yes, yes. Very well. (Looking out front.) What a remarkably pretty clock! (He enters inn.)
TRUFFALDINO	Yes, it's lovely, sir. (With utmost speed.) For what we are about to receive may nothing stand in the way. (He dives into the inn.)

Scene Seventeen

A room in the house of PANTALONE. CLARICE and PANTALONE talking off-stage before entering together.

PANTALONE	Daughter, daughter, I'll not be bamboozled - I'il not be undermined by sentiment. You'll marry Federigo. I've given my word. It's as simple as that.
CLARICE	I'll not marry Signor Federigo.
PANTALONE	Oh dear, oh dear, what's a man to do? Look, daughter, this Signor Federigo is a pleasant enough chap surely?
CLARICE	Not to me.
PANTALONE	Why not?
CLARICE	I hate him.
PANTALONE	Hate him? Nonsense. You just get that Silvio out of your noddle and you'll soon find that Signor Federigo is the finest figure of a husband any girl could wish for.
CLARICE	I'll not forget Silvio - I love him.
PANTALONE	I'm not talking of love - I'm talking of marriage.
	(CLARICE howls.)
	Oh, shut up, please. I'll not have my heart softened by you or anybody.

Scene Eighteen

The same. SMERALDINA enters down steps and stops half-way.

SMERALDINA   Sir! Master! Signor Pantalone!

PANTALONE   Yes? What is it?

SMERALDINA   Signor Federigo is here. He wishes to speak
with you.

PANTALONE   Show him in.

(SMERALDINA goes out again. CLARICE howls.)

Come on, daughter. Less of the fairy fountains
for heaven's sake.

CLARICE   But, father please!

PANTALONE   (giving her a handkerchief)   Have a good blow.

Scene Nineteen

The same. SMERALDINA enters followed by BEATRICE down steps.

SMERALDINA   Signor Federigo Rasponi.   (She goes out.)

PANTALONE   (to CLARICE)   Your husband's here.

BEATRICE   Signor Pantalone.

PANTALONE   (to BEATRICE)   My respects, sir.

(CLARICE sobs.)

BEATRICE   Your daughter, sir - why is she sobbing?

PANTALONE   Why? Well, shall we say the news of your
death has left a lasting impression.

BEATRICE   Signor Pantalone, do something for me. Leave
                  me alone with her for a while. I might be able
                  to comfort her.

PANTALONE   Very well.   (Aside.)   I'll try anything.
                  Daughter, your husband-to-be would speak to you
                  in private.

                  (CLARICE howls.)

                  She's all yours, sir. I'll take my leave.   (He
                  bows and leaves.)

                  Scene Twenty

The same.

CLARICE   Oh, I'll not marry! Never! Not even if they
                  drag me to the altar!

BEATRICE   (aside)   I have not the heart to see her suffer
                  so. I shall tell her all immediately.   (Coughs)
                  There is something I must confide.   Clarice!
                  You do not want me and neither do I want you!

CLARICE   What?

BEATRICE   Even if you proffered yourself to me I wouldn't
                  know what to do with you.

CLARICE   I don't understand.

BEATRICE   You love another. So do I.

CLARICE   You do?

BEATRICE   Yes. Prepare yourself for a surprise.

CLARICE	What is it?
BEATRICE	I am not Federigo Rasponi.
CLARICE	Not?
BEATRICE	I am Beatrice, his sister.
CLARICE	Sister? What are you saying? You are a woman?
BEATRICE	Indeed I am. Every inch a woman.
CLARICE	Oh! How can you stand there and torment me?
BEATRICE	You don't believe I am a woman. Very well, since you insist, I shall give you proof.
CLARICE	Proof?
BEATRICE	Yes, my dear. (Turns U. S. apparently about to open trousers.)
CLARICE	Oh! Oh, I believe you.
BEATRICE	Ah.
CLARICE	Oh! But your brother? What is the truth about your brother?
BEATRICE	My brother is dead.
CLARICE	Oh good! Oh!
BEATRICE	He was killed by my lover, who has disappeared. I am trying to trace him, wearing this disguise. I have confided this secret because I could not bear to see you so affected, but I beg you by all the sacred laws of friendship, do not betray me.
CLARICE	Never.
BEATRICE	You are on your honour to tell no one.
CLARICE	Oh, I promise, on my honour. None. Silvio?
BEATRICE	No, I forbid it. The fewer who know the better.
CLARICE	Well then, I shan't say a word.
BEATRICE	Thank you. Well now, are we not friends?

CLARICE	Indeed we are, and if ever I can be of any help, you have only to command me.
BEATRICE	And I too swear eternal friendship.

Scene Twenty-one

The same. PANTALONE enters and sees them.

BEATRICE	Give me your hand as a sign of your love and loyalty.
CLARICE	Most gladly.
BEATRICE	You'll not break your promise to me?
CLARICE	I take my oath on it.
	(They kiss each other on both cheeks.)
PANTALONE	Promise? Oath? Kisses! What's this? And so soon! Bravo! You're a bit of a speedy worker, aren't you? Well, there's one thing quite clear to me now, we must get you two married immediately.
CLARICE	Married!
BEATRICE	There's no need for such haste, sir, I do assure you.
PANTALONE	Oh, isn't there? I can see the twinkle in your eye, m'boy!
CLARICE	But, father!
PANTALONE	Hush, girl. You needn't be so shamefaced. Daddy understands. You're both in a hurry so the wedding will be tomorrow. Oh, yes, we

don't want any disturbances in church, do we, so I'll just go and have a word with Signor Silvio. Make him understand.

CLARICE   Oh father, keep him calm! Don't let him desert me.

PANTALONE   Desert you? You don't want two husbands, do you? Greedy guts! Ha, ha, ha, I'll be back presently. As you were, Federigo.   (He goes out.)

CLARICE   (to BEATRICE)   Oh, now you've made things worse than ever.

(Music. BEATRICE and CLARICE go out.)

Scene Twenty-two

The courtyard. SILVIO comes in with drawn sword and comes down to the house of PANTALONE. The DOCTOR appears and the Music fades as he speaks.

DOCTOR   Silvio, my boy, what are you doing?

SILVIO   Oh, father. I am outraged! I am humiliated! I am slighted. I am affronted!

DOCTOR   Hold your temper. Don't be so hasty, lad.

SILVIO   But Pantalone must give me satisfaction.

DOCTOR   Leave him to me. I'll deal with it.

SILVIO   But, father –

DOCTOR   Obedience, my boy! Do as I say!

SILVIO   Very well, father, I'll obey you.   (He moves to leave, then turns.)   But, father, as the

	name of our family is sacred to us, should Signor Pantalone persist in his insult, then I shall deal with him. Death is the only answer! (He goes out.)
DOCTOR	Oh, my poor boy! How I pity him! _Damnum sine injuria!_ How he suffers without remedy! However, the law is on my side. My son shall marry Pantalone's daughter. (There is a noise off-stage.) Aha! I shall now inform Signor Pantalone of his legal obligations.

(PANTALONE enters and crosses in front of DOCTOR.)

Aha!

(PANTALONE jumps and turns to see the DOCTOR.)

The man with whom I wish to speak. |
PANTALONE	Ah, Doctor, I was just on my way to visit you.
DOCTOR	You are going to assure me that after all your daughter will be marrying my Silvio.
PANTALONE	But look, sir, my daughter is in love with –
DOCTOR	With my son – exactly. Now let me put you right concerning the law.
PANTALONE	The law?
DOCTOR	The law on marriage is absolutely plain and straightforward. It is, in a nutshell – _consensus et non concubitus fecit verum._
PANTALONE	Eh?
DOCTOR	Latin.
PANTALONE	But I don't know Latin.
DOCTOR	It means your daughter is free to choose the man she loves. The law will uphold her. The wishes of the daughter are paramount.
PANTALONE	They are?

DOCTOR	They are.
PANTALONE	Anything else to say?
DOCTOR	I've said my last word.
PANTALONE	Finished?
DOCTOR	Finished.
PANTALONE	My dear Doctor –
DOCTOR	And don't you worry about the dowry. It's not your money I'm after, I assure you.
PANTALONE	Shall we start again?
DOCTOR	Eh?
PANTALONE	My turn now?
DOCTOR	Your turn.
PANTALONE	You say that all my attempts to give Signor Federigo to my daughter will come to nothing if she should not love him?
DOCTOR	Exactly. I could not have put it better myself.
PANTALONE	Fancy that! And I don't speak Latin!
	(Both laugh.)
	Well, let me inform you, sir, that he has captured her heart.
DOCTOR	Who?
PANTALONE	Federigo Rasponi.
DOCTOR	Federigo Rasponi?
PANTALONE	I have just left them in there, exchanging promises, oaths and fond embraces.
DOCTOR	But only this morning she was in love with my son. Oh, it's shameless!
PANTALONE	You're not casting aspersions against my daughter, I hope?

DOCTOR

Not against your daughter - against you - you! How have you achieved it then? Threats? Intimidation? Menaces? Oh, there are laws against all that, I'll tell you. I'll have an injunction set against the marriage. I'll have you sued for breaking of contracts, breach of promise - blackmail of daughters - public slander of my family. Nemo non hat habet - dunc!   (He goes.)

PANTALONE

You do what you like, I'm not afraid of you. (To audience.)   My daughter's going to marry a Rasponi, God bless her! A Rasponi in the family! The Rasponis have got quality, and they've got riches! Do you think I'd let her marry a Lombardi when she has a chance like this?

(SILVIO enters with drawn sword, unseen by PANTALONE.)

One Rasponi is worth a thousand Lombardis!

SILVIO

What's that you say?

PANTALONE

One Rasponi is worth a thousand Lombardis - (He turns and sees SILVIO.)   Oh!

SILVIO

Then know, sir, that I, Silvio Ottavio Pietro Antonio Giovanni, youngest son of the thrice illustrious house of the Lombardis, do demand of you, sir, instant satisfaction. Now draw, sirrah, draw!

PANTALONE

(tugging at his stick)   But it doesn't draw!

SILVIO

Oh, do be quick about it, sir. This hand of mine is itching to run you through. Now draw, I say!

PANTALONE

Oh heavens!   (He draws a pistol out of his pocket.)

SILVIO

Oh, so that's it, is it? A pistol against a sword. The odds are all on your side, sirrah, but a Lombardi, sir, is no coward, no he is not, so

I'll still take you on. Set to!

PANTALONE   (with trembling hand trying to pull back the
                     hammer)   Oh God, how does it work?

Scene Twenty-three

The same. BEATRICE dashes on with sheathed swordstick in hand.

BEATRICE   Stay! Father-in-law, I beg you, grant me the
                    honour of taking up this challenge.

PANTALONE   Granted.

BEATRICE   Or would you rather kill him yourself?

PANTALONE   No. You go ahead.

BEATRICE   On guard, Lombardi!

SILVIO   A pleasure, Rasponi!

BEATRICE   I warn you, sir, I have been taught by the best
                    fencing masters in Turin. Care to think again?

SILVIO   Never! To hell with Turin and all the Rasponis,
                    say I!

                    (PANTALONE fires pistol. SILVIO falls to
                    ground in surprise.)

PANTALONE   (staggering about)   It worked! It worked!

                    (BEATRICE and SILVIO start fighting. SILVIO
                    lunges forward, PANTALONE getting in the way,
                    whereupon SILVIO chases him off.)

                    Help, help! Not me - him! Help! Not me - him!

                    (SILVIO and BEATRICE fight. BEATRICE knocks
                    his sword out of his hand and points hers at his
                    throat.)

Scene Twenty-four

The same. CLARICE rushes to L. of BEATRICE.

CLARICE	Stop! Stop! Don't!
BEATRICE	He challenged the house of Rasponi!
CLARICE	Oh no, please.
BEATRICE	You would have me spare his life?
CLARICE	I beg you.
BEATRICE	You in return will remember your promise to me?
CLARICE	I swear.
BEATRICE	(to SILVIO) Well, Silvio Lombardi - you're a lucky fellow! Be grateful to her! (BEATRICE marches off stage quickly.)

Scene Twenty-five

The same.

CLARICE	(rushing to SILVIO) Oh, my darling Silvio! Are you safe?
SILVIO	You deceiver.
CLARICE	What?
SILVIO	This oath that you have just sworn - what is it?
CLARICE	Oh, forgive me. I can't tell. I promised secrecy.
SILVIO	With him? So! We have it now. You little cheat! You little fraud! You little Jezebel!
CLARICE	I shall die if you go on like this!
SILVIO	Then die! Because I would rather see you dead than lead a life of lies.

CLARICE (picking up his sword)   Very well! If that's
what you want, I'll die.   (Pointing the sword
to her breast.)   One day you'll know how much
I loved you! Sword, come!

Scene Twenty-six

The same. SMERALDINA rushes on with basket of vegetables.

SMERALDINA What! What the devil you doin'?   (She
snatches the sword from CLARICE. Then to
SILVIO.)   Drive her to this, would you? To
hell with you, that's what I say. Go on! Clear
off! Rubbish!

(CLARICE bursts into tears and rushes off.)

Scene Twenty-seven

The same.

SMERALDINA What do you think you're at then? Stand by?
Let her do herself in?

SILVIO But it was all a pretence. She's a two-faced
perfidious wretch.

SMERALDINA   Oh, go calling her names now, will we? I know
                 your game. Soon as a woman starts having a
                 mind of her own you men start ruining her
                 reputation.

SILVIO   That's not true.

SMERALDINA   It's all very well for you men to invent
                 scandalous tales about women. When given half
                 the chance, you're off committing all the
                 infidelities you can. Why are we women always
                 condemned - and why are you men always
                 excused? I'll tell you why; 'cos the laws are
                 made by them men. I mean, if women made the
                 laws, things'd be different. All right, if I
                 ruled, I'd put every man what's unfaithful up to
                 public show, I would. I'd make him carry an oak
                 branch in his hands. Second thoughts, perhaps
                 not. Do that and we wouldn't be able to move for
                 trees, would we?   (As if she's going to be
                 sick.)   You men!   (She goes off.)

                 Scene Twenty-eight

The same. Music. SILVIO is alone.

SILVIO   Oh, Clarice, you have deceived me! I must be
                 revenged. Fate did make me stumble before my
                 rival. Yet in spite of fate, all my thoughts are
                 vengeance. Federigo shall die. Yes, Clarice,
                 when next you see your lover, he will be
                 steeped in his own blood! I swear it!
                 (He leaves.)

                 (Music fades.)

Scene Twenty-nine

At the inn. TRUFFALDINO enters.

TRUFFALDINO	You'd never believe it – two masters and none of 'em's had their dinner yet. Of course, you know what will happen, don't you? They'll both want serving at the same time. I'll be in a right mess then.
	(BEATRICE enters.)
BEATRICE	Ah, there you are, Truffaldino. I'm ready for dinner.
TRUFFALDINO	Everything comes to him who waits!
BEATRICE	Tell the innkeeper I'll want a table for two. I've asked Signor Pantalone to join me.
TRUFFALDINO	And what would you like to eat, sir?
BEATRICE	Oh, I don't know. Not a lot. Quality rather than quantity, I think.
TRUFFALDINO	Why not leave the ordering to me, sir?
BEATRICE	Oh?
TRUFFALDINO	I'm a bit of an expert in the food line, sir.
BEATRICE	Well, why not? You go ahead. Excel yourself.
TRUFFALDINO	Do you mean a bit of the old Haute Cuisine, sir?
BEATRICE	Exactly.
TRUFFALDINO	You can have the utmost confidence in me, sir.
	(BEATRICE nods, and rings bell at door.)
	(To audience.) I can order what I like! What do I fancy? What do I fancy?
BEATRICE	(turning back) A moment!
TRUFFALDINO	He's gone off his food again! Yes, sir?
BEATRICE	Take this banker's order, will you, (Hands it to him.) and put it in my trunk. Now be

	careful with it. It is a letter of credit for four thousand crowns.
TRUFFALDINO	Don't worry. Everything's safe with me, sir.
BEATRICE	Then I shall leave everything to you. I won't be long.
	(SMERALDINA ushers BEATRICE off. TRUFFALDINO sees her and greets her saucily. She reacts and goes out, leaving TRUFFALDINO alone.)
TRUFFALDINO	(to SMERALDINA) Hey up! (To audience.) Now's my chance to impress him with my taste and discernment. You didn't think I could be gastronomical, did you? Let me tell you, I've had many a master what's gourmetted themselves. The problem, though, is this banker's note. Still, I can always pop it in his trunk later. There's no time to lose. Food's calling! Brighella! Brighella! (He goes out.)

Scene Thirty

The same. TRUFFALDINO re-enters. BRIGHELLA then enters.

TRUFFALDINO	Brighella!
BRIGHELLA	You called me, did you?
TRUFFALDINO	I did.
BRIGHELLA	What do you want?
TRUFFALDINO	My master is entertaining a friend for lunch. He knows I'm a bit of a connoisseur in these matters, and he's left the table arrangements

to me.

BRIGHELLA	Oh, very well, then.
TRUFFALDINO	Now then. I want the best table you've got.
BRIGHELLA	I'll have you know this is a first class establishment. All my special guests eat in private rooms. I'll put your master and his guest in there. (Pointing off.)
TRUFFALDINO	Now what can we have to eat?
BRIGHELLA	For two persons - two courses - four dishes each.
TRUFFALDINO	My master asked for five or six - so we'd better make it seven or eight. (To audience.) Seven or eight, eh?
BRIGHELLA	Something special, perhaps?
TRUFFALDINO	Something special, naturally.
BRIGHELLA	Well, as a first course, may I recommend my gazpacho andalus con cerezas.
TRUFFALDINO	Oh yeth - and wath that?
BRIGHELLA	Cold Spanish soup with cherries. Then I can offer a choice of my pasta or my fish, or my fricassee, and to finish off with, you shall have my pudden.
TRUFFALDINO	I beg your pardon?
BRIGHELLA	I said, to finish off with, you shall have my pudden.
TRUFFALDINO	Say Pooding.
BRIGHELLA	No. Pudden.
TRUFFALDINO	Say POOO.
BRIGHELLA	POOO.
TRUFFALDINO	DINNGG.
BRIGHELLA	DINNNGG.

TRUFFALDINO	GGE.
BRIGHELLA	GGE.
TRUFFALDINO	POOODINNNGE.
BRIGHELLA	Pudden.
TRUFFALDINO	What is it, anyway?
BRIGHELLA	It's an English dish. And I'll have you know that people come from miles around, just to gaze at my pudden.
TRUFFALDINO	Do they really? What about the laying of the table?
BRIGHELLA	Oh, I leave that to the waiters.
TRUFFALDINO	Oh no, you don't. The laying of the table is the very first ingredient. Everything depends on it. Allow me to demonstrate the laying of a table. (Starts to mime laying the table.) Get hold of that.
BRIGHELLA	Get hold of what?
TRUFFALDINO	The table.
	(TRUFFALDINO and BRIGHELLA mime picking up heavy table and moving it D.C. TRUFFALDINO then picks up imaginary table cloth and spreads it over imaginary table. Music. TRUFFALDINO smoothes down table cloth and gestures to BRIGHELLA who drops corner of table cloth neatly into place. TRUFFALDINO goes to table L. and brings back imaginary cruet and places it on table.)
	Condiments - salt - pepper - mustard.
	(He holds up three fingers. So does BRIGHELLA. TRUFFALDINO goes to table and gets knife.)
	Knife. (Goes back to table L. and returns holding up another knife.) Guess what?
BRIGHELLA	Another knife.

(TRUFFALDINO puts second knife on table and
goes back to table L. to get a fork.)

TRUFFALDINO   Fork.   (He puts it down and goes back to table
L.)   And another.

(He brings back another fork but drops it. Bends
down to pick it up and bangs his head on table.
BRIGHELLA picks it up and rubs it clean.
TRUFFALDINO gestures BRIGHELLA to put it
on table. BRIGHELLA does so. TRUFFALDINO
then moves it slightly.)

The table is laid. Now where do we put the
food?

BRIGHELLA   Ah, the food.

(He lays out the food in a balletic fashion,
TRUFFALDINO reacting as required.)

I puts my meat here.   (Puts it on table from
above it.)   My taters here.   (Puts it at
top L. corner.)   My carrots I put here.
(He trips round L. end of table, holding carrots
high and does ballet jump when over at L.)
And my peas –   (He walks into bottom R.
corner of table and hurts himself.)

TRUFFALDINO   Yes, it does bring the water to your eyes.

(Music fades here and the rest of the mime is
done without music.)

BRIGHELLA   (walking as though in pain)   And my peas I put
here.   (He puts them down from above table.)

TRUFFALDINO   Meat – potatoes – carrots – peas. And what
goes in the middle, please?

BRIGHELLA   (miming it as he speaks)   In the middle I puts
– my pudden.

(Both greet this with rapture. But then
TRUFFALDINO changes his mind.)

TRUFFALDINO   Wrong. The meat goes in the middle.

(They start to argue and to walk and bump into table and finally round it to come to the centre of the stage, still arguing.)

There's the taters, carrots, peas, pudden and the meat goes in the middle.

(They kneel down and to demonstrate his point TRUFFALDINO starts tearing up the banknote, putting the bits in various places on the ground.)

Scene Thirty-one

The same. BEATRICE and PANTALONE enter and come behind them. Both have hats and sticks.

BEATRICE	What have you done to my banknote?
TRUFFALDINO	(in horror) Banknote?
	(BRIGHELLA gets up and breaks R. TRUFFALDINO starts picking up the bits.)
BEATRICE	So that's the way you look after my things, is it?
TRUFFALDINO	(picking up bits) Don't worry, sir. I can always stick it together again.
BEATRICE	You deserve a good beating. Don't you think so, Signor Pantalone?
PANTALONE	Don't worry. I can always write you out another one.
TRUFFALDINO	It's not my fault, sir. I was only demonstrating my table arrangements.
BEATRICE	(giving TRUFFALDINO both sticks - her hat in

his hand and PANTALONE's hat on his head
which goes down over his eyes)   You've
got excuses for everything. Now then, off with
you.

(TRUFFALDINO exits with hats and sticks.)

PANTALONE   I really don't understand that chap, you know.
Sometimes he's as shrewd as they make them,
other times, you couldn't think of a bigger fool.

BEATRICE   He acts stupid on purpose, the rogue.
(To BRIGHELLA.)   Well now, is dinner
ready?

BRIGHELLA   Well, if you're going to have seven dishes for
each course, it's going to take a bit of time, I'm
afraid.

BEATRICE   What's all this about seven dishes? If you'll
allow me, sir, we'll take pot luck - a soup and a
couple of dishes - my tastes are simple.

BRIGHELLA   Very good. Is there anything particular that you
fancy, sir?

PANTALONE   I'd like some meat balls if you have them.   My
teeth are not very good nowadays.

BRIGHELLA   (peering at PANTALONE's teeth)   No, they're
not, sir, are they? If you'll stay here, dinner
will be ready directly.   (He moves towards
inn.)

BEATRICE   Tell Truffaldino to wait on us.

BRIGHELLA   Yes, I'll tell him.   (He pulls back folding
shutters from serving hatch, and goes off.)

Scene Thirty-two

The same.

PANTALONE	It is most kind of you, Signor, to take me out to luncheon.
BEATRICE	Not at all, Signor. Think of tomorrow. Tomorrow I shall wed your daughter.
PANTALONE	Ah, I could not have given her to a more manly man - the power of your sword, your looks, and if I may say so, sir, your riches; you have it all, sir, you have it all.
	(BRIGHELLA enters, followed by FAT WAITER who carries very large tray with two place settings and the check pudding-cloth on it. He has a table-cloth over arm. Second comes YOUNG WAITER with smaller tray on which he has bread, jug of wine and two glasses. Finally comes OLD WAITER with very small tray with silver vase and one rose on it.)
BRIGHELLA	Come along, then. This way. Lay the table.
	(The WAITERS cross in line in front of him on their way out.)
PANTALONE	They're very quick about their business here.
BRIGHELLA	(as OLD WAITER crawls past him) Oh, they're like lightning, sir, like lightning. (He helps OLD WAITER on his way with a kick and then goes out.)

Scene Thirty-three

The same. Music.

PANTALONE

In my younger days I used to dine at a lovely
little place along the Grand Canal, facing the
Rialto. I used to eat there with my friends.
What times we had. Such wines, such
exquisite dishes! Oh, had you but known that
company. Such hearts - sincerity, openness,
truth. We talked and we talked - we thrashed it
all out - we were young then. Why isn't it the
same now? It should be better. I'm older,
wiser - and I've got more money. Why has it all
gone? Gone. It'll come back. My daughter off
my hands. I'll be gone again. Young!

(Music fades.)

(During this speech the three waiters have
re-entered. FAT WAITER and YOUNG WAITER
have set the table in the centre of the stage. The
OLD WAITER goes off and is seen putting tray on
the hatch. This tray has four dessert plates on
top of which are two clean soup plates, one
plate of grated cheese, one plate of croutons
and also one table spoon. FAT WAITER puts
table cloth on tables and places red check
pudding cloth at one end and then fetches tray,
the contents of which he then lays on the table.
All the waiters have gone off stage by the end of
PANTALONE's speech.)

Scene Thirty-four

The same. TRUFFALDINO enters with enormous tureen half-full of
thick green-pea soup with ladle in it. He has table-spoon in his pocket.

TRUFFALDINO	Soup? Would you kindly oblige me by taking your seats in the other room, sir, with your spoons at the ready. (He puts the tureen on the table.)
BEATRICE	Go and put the soup on the table.
TRUFFALDINO	After you, sir.
PANTALONE	(moving to leave) I suppose we'd better humour this strange servant of yours.
BEATRICE	(following him, then turning back to TRUFFALDINO) I want less foolery and more service, understand?
	(BEATRICE and PANTALONE go out.)
TRUFFALDINO	Always a privilege and always a pleasure, sir. (Picking up the crouton and cheese plates, then the two clean soup plates, waiter fashion, on his left arm and in his left hand. To audience.) No taste - no discernment! After all the trouble I've taken over his cold Spanish soup with cherries, what does he end up with? Pea soup and crumbs! I ask you! Look at that! (Picks up a ladle full of the green pea soup and lets it slop back into the tureen, then fills both soup plates half-full and comes L. of table, still talking to audience.) Oh well, I suppose I'd better taste it for them. (Takes table-spoon out of pocket.) Always got my spoon at the ready. (Has two tastes.) Mmmmm - lovely.
BEATRICE	(off stage) Truffaldino!
TRUFFALDINO	Coming, sir. On the pea soup! (And he goes out with all four plates.)

(YOUNG WAITER enters with covered dish containing Lasagne Bolognese with a fork sticking in it.)

YOUNG WAITER   Where's the Truffaldino chap? I thought he wanted to serve. Oh well, I'll do it myself.

(TRUFFALDINO enters empty-handed and moves to R. of YOUNG WAITER.)

TRUFFALDINO   What's this?

YOUNG WAITER   (lifting lid and offering dish)   Lasagne Bolognese!

TRUFFALDINO   (taking dish)   It looks like lasagne - it smells like lasagne -   (Taking forkful and biting.) and, by golly, it tastes like lasagne. On the lasagne!

(YOUNG WAITER takes soup tureen from table and goes out with tureen and lasagne lid. TRUFFALDINO sets off to serve the lasagne. Just as he gets near the door FLORINDO enters with hat and stick and moves to L. of table.)

FLORINDO   Truffaldino!

TRUFFALDINO   (turning)   Sir?

FLORINDO   Where are you going with that dish?

TRUFFALDINO   I was just about to put it on the table, sir.

FLORINDO   Who's it for?

TRUFFALDINO   For you, sir.

FLORINDO   Why are you putting it on the table before you knew I was back in the house?

TRUFFALDINO   Er - I saw you through the window, sir.

FLORINDO   You were quick, weren't you?

TRUFFALDINO   Always my anxiety to please, sir.

FLORINDO   Haven't you made a mistake?

TRUFFALDINO   Sir?

FLORINDO	What is that curious-looking stuff? Lasagne, isn't it?
TRUFFALDINO	Yes, sir.
FLORINDO	Yes, I thought it was. Then why are you bringing me the lasagne before the soup?
TRUFFALDINO	In Venice, sir, we have the soup last.
FLORINDO	Indeed.
TRUFFALDINO	It's very much the custom - very much de rigueur, sir.
FLORINDO	Be that as it may. I'll have my soup first. Take that lasagne back into the kitchen and bring me my soup.

(FLORINDO crosses R. below table for room where BEATRICE and PANTALONE are. TRUFFALDINO goes to other side.)

Tell me, Truffaldino, where do I have my meals? Is it in here?   (Pointing off.)

TRUFFALDINO	(yells) No!

(FLORINDO turns in a surprised manner and TRUFFALDINO speaks very softly.)

I mean 'no' - you eat in here, sir.   (Pointing other way.)

FLORINDO	(crossing below table) Oh, very well.
TRUFFALDINO	What would you like to order, sir?
FLORINDO	Oh, leave that to the innkeeper. Let him provide of his best. (To audience.) Do you know, I've been to the post office and I can't find out where Beatrice is staying. Oh well, I'd better keep up my spirits. Still, a good meal might help. Yes, that's it. Eat, and live in hope.

(During this TRUFFALDINO has been tiptoeing across with the dish of lasagne. FLORINDO turns and sees him.)

Truffaldino! Take that lasagne back into the kitchen and bring me my soup!   (He goes out.)

TRUFFALDINO   (to audience)   I've got one master in here and one master in there. If I pull this off it really will be something to boast of.   (As he goes out.)   On the lasagne!

(He goes with dish and we hear voice of BEATRICE off stage.)

BEATRICE   Thank you, Truffaldino, that looks delicious.

(OLD WAITER and YOUNG WAITER enter. OLD WAITER carries fish dish with lid.)

OLD WAITER   Truffaldino? Where is he?

YOUNG WAITER   He's not here. Right. I'll take it.

(OLD WAITER and YOUNG WAITER both tug at dish. TRUFFALDINO enters empty-handed.)

TRUFFALDINO   Hey, just a minute. What's this?

OLD WAITER   (lifting lid and handing it to YOUNG WAITER) River trout with Bearnaise sauce.

TRUFFALDINO   (taking it)   River trout with Bearnaise sauce!

(TRUFFALDINO goes above table and puts fish down. OLD WAITER goes out. YOUNG WAITER stands, holding lid.

(To YOUNG WAITER.)   Don't just stand there. There's a gentleman waiting to get his soup down him.

YOUNG WAITER   Right.   (Starting to go.)   I'll serve him at once.

TRUFFALDINO   I said lay the table. I'll do the serving.

(OLD WAITER has re-entered with small tray. On it are two fish knives and one fish fork.)

YOUNG WAITER   (as he goes)   Please yourself.

(Music. OLD WAITER comes down to L. of
TRUFFALDINO with small tray. They both bend
down and smell fish and straighten up again.
TRUFFALDINO lifts right arm above his head.
TRUFFALDINO takes knife from tray held by
OLD WAITER and makes cut in fish.
NOTE: Fish has base stuck to dish. Then bone
with head and tail. Then top part divided in two
down line of bone.
TRUFFALDINO gets squirt of juice in eye. He
rubs it having put knife down; he brings right
hand above his head again. TRUFFALDINO
takes second knife and makes another cut. This
time juice squirts into OLD WAITER's eye.
TRUFFALDINO mops it for him. TRUFFALDINO
brings up right hand again. TRUFFALDINO
takes fork from tray - separates fish from bone,
and finishes with bone in hand by end of phrase of
music. He and the OLD WAITER bow to each
other and OLD WAITER goes out with tray.
TRUFFALDINO comes D.C. playing fish bone
like a mouth organ, and humming 'Santa Lucia'.
As he does this, enter FAT WAITER with large
tray, YOUNG WAITER with medium tray and
OLD WAITER with small tray plus vase and rose,
all three of them exactly as they were when they
made their first entrance at the beginning of
banquet. They stand in line L. of table, gazing
in astonishment at TRUFFALDINO.)

TRUFFALDINO   Come on, don't just stand there. Get the table
laid up. There's a gentleman waiting for his
soup in there.

(The three WAITERS go out with their trays.
TRUFFALDINO hooks fish bone on to back of
OLD WAITER as he goes. TRUFFALDINO picks
up the fish.)

On the river trout with the Bearnaise sauce!
(He goes.)

(Re-enter OLD WAITER with small tray and

YOUNG WAITER with duplicate medium tray - empty.)

OLD WAITER   Funny chap, that! He seems to want to serve here, there and everywhere.

YOUNG WAITER   What do I care so long as I get my tip? Come on, I'll race you back to the kitchen.

(OLD WAITER and YOUNG WAITER go out. Re-enter TRUFFALDINO carrying one clean soup plate and one breakable, plaster of paris plate.)

TRUFFALDINO   (crossing)   On the pea soup!

(This phrase is echoed off stage by all three WAITERS. TRUFFALDINO drops breakable plate and bends down to clear up.)

Anyone got a dustpan and brush? Look at all this mess.

(He goes on muttering about the mess, while at the same time all three WAITERS are calling off stage 'Red hot', 'Red hot', 'Red hot'. YOUNG WAITER enters and dumps duplicate soup tureen down. TRUFFALDINO straightens up, picking it up and throwing it off stage. There is a noisy crockery crash off stage. Almost at once FAT WAITER comes in with pea soup all over his head and apron. He comes to R. of TRUFFALDINO. TRUFFALDINO takes empty soup plate which he had placed on floor, gets spoon out of his pocket and scrapes soup off FAT WAITER into soup plate.

Service with a smile.   (Goes off with soup plate.)   On the pea soup.

FLORINDO   (off stage)   Thank you, Truffaldino, what delicious soup.

(FAT WAITER goes off. YOUNG WAITER enters with fricassee dish and lid. Fricassee dish has edible peas scattered over it. YOUNG WAITER

crosses TRUFFALDINO who has re-entered.
TRUFFALDINO turns to YOUNG WAITER.)

TRUFFALDINO	What's this?
YOUNG WAITER	(lifting lid) Fricassee.
TRUFFALDINO	Fricawhat? (Taking dish.)
YOUNG WAITER	Fricassee.
TRUFFALDINO	(picking up a pea) Ah, a pea. (Sings final phrase of 'Song of the Flea'.) Ha, ha, ha, ha – ha, ha, ha, ha. I love a big fat pea.

(YOUNG WAITER puts lid on floor and applauds.
Enter FAT WAITER. TRUFFALDINO sings à la
Figaro.)

Fricassee.

(FAT and YOUNG WAITERS stand in oblique line
L. of table and applaud. Enter OLD WAITER to
join the line. TRUFFALDINO sings.)

Fricassee.

(All three WAITERS applaud.)

Fricassee – Fricassee – Fricassee – Fricassee.

BEATRICE	(off stage) Truffaldino!
FLORINDO	(off stage) Truffaldino!

(Music – Figaro.)

TRUFFALDINO	(sings) Fricassee here. (Gesturing R.)
WAITERS	(singing) Fricassee there. (Gesturing L.)

(This repeats to the music. TRUFFALDINO
gets angry and throws peas at the WAITERS. He
sings his next line on the last phrase of the music.)

TRUFFALDINO	(sings) What do you mean – what do you mean – what do you mean?

(WAITERS rush off in fury. On last four chords
TRUFFALDINO does knees bend, then takes

fricassee dish to go out. As he goes.)

On the fricassee!

BEATRICE   (off stage)   Thank you, Truffaldino.

(OLD WAITER has come in with big dish of trick spaghetti. He has loose end tucked under his arm. TRUFFALDINO re-enters.)

TRUFFALDINO   What's this?

OLD WAITER   Spaghetti.

(Music. TRUFFALDINO takes dish and crosses. Spaghetti starts unwinding.)

BEATRICE   (off stage)   Truffaldino!

TRUFFALDINO   Sir.   (And he winds spaghetti round OLD WAITER as he crosses him to answer BEATRICE.)

FLORINDO   (off stage)   Truffaldino!

(And more spaghetti is wound round the OLD WAITER. BEATRICE and FLORINDO each call off stage once more. By this time OLD WAITER is tightly wound in spaghetti. The rest drops off the dish as TRUFFALDINO moves off. He unwinds OLD WAITER by spinning him round, picks up rest of spaghetti and goes out. Returns at once with spaghetti tray, bumps into OLD WAITER, handing him the tray and spinning him to the side where the tray is handed out. YOUNG WAITER enters with lidded dish of meat balls, small rubber balls painted brown.)

YOUNG WAITER   (taking off lid)   Here - take these meat balls to your master.

(TRUFFALDINO takes three of the meat balls and juggles with them. YOUNG WAITER goes out with dish and lid.)

BEATRICE   (off stage)   Truffaldino!

(TRUFFALDINO bounces a ball, takes spoon out

of pocket and goes out with meatball in spoon.)

TRUFFALDINO   (as he goes)   On the meatballs!

(At once FAT WAITER enters with big pudding
on wheels, staggering across stage and then D. S.
with it. TRUFFALDINO re-enters with pile of
trick plates and one breakable plate on top. He
staggers with them to OLD WAITER, bumps into
him and knocks him to the ground.
TRUFFALDINO then drops breakable plate and
staggers along stage seeming about to throw the
plates into the audience. While all eyes are on
TRUFFALDINO, the OLD WAITER hooks string
that runs off stage on to the hook on the pudding,
in preparation for business at end of scene.
TRUFFALDINO reels round stage with plates,
finally throwing them off L. There is a very
loud crockery crash off. The OLD WAITER has
gone off by now. Music fades on the crash.
TRUFFALDINO comes to pudding and looks at it.)

If they think they're going to have any of that,
they've got another think coming. That is for
me later.   (He takes check cloth from table,
originally placed there by FAT WAITER when he
laid the table cloth at the beginning of banquet.
Check cloth is used to cover pudding.)   The
pudding's off, and we're on the flambée.

(The three WAITERS enter and repeat his shout
'on the flambée'. TRUFFALDINO sings à la
Figaro.)

Flamboe.

WAITERS   (sing)   Flambée.

(FAT WAITER carries a lit burner and YOUNG
WAITER a trick frying-pan. OLD WAITER
carries a tray with No. 2 liquid in bottle, spoon,
small dish chips of dry ice and seven paper
plates, the top one of which has cotton wool
stuck to it.
NOTE: Trick frying-pan. This has small

cylinder for blowing up white balloon, two
electrical charges for flash and exploding
balloon and No. 1 liquid in pan. All these are
worked on cue by FAT WAITER.)

TRUFFALDINO   (sings)   Flambée.

WAITERS   (bringing things down to TRUFFALDINO who is
above table. FAT WAITER puts burner down.
YOUNG WAITER puts frying pan on burner.
They sing in reply.)   Flambée.

(Music - Figaro.)

TRUFFALDINO   (singing)   Flambée here.

(OLD WAITER hands bottle to TRUFFALDINO,
who pours liquid into pan and tips in the dry ice.)

WAITERS   (singing)   Flambée there.

TRUFFALDINO   (singing)   Brandy here.

WAITERS   (singing)   Brandy there.

ALL   (singing)   Mix it up - mix it up - mix it in -
mix it in - mix it in.   (Continuing trend of
phrase to music.)

(While this is going on, the two liquids have
combined to make foam in the frying pan - the
dry ice is sending out puffs of smoke - the FAT
WAITER has pulled the string releasing air from
cylinder which blows up the balloon on the frying
pan. TRUFFALDINO is mixing it all up as he
and the WAITERS sing. On the end of the phrase
where TRUFFALDINO did his knees bend in the
'Fricassee' sequence, FAT WAITER presses the
switch on the frying pan which releases the
electric charges and there is a flash and the
balloon explodes. They all jump back startled.
Then TRUFFALDINO spoons some foam from
frying pan, and goes out with it. Meanwhile,
the FAT WAITER has picked up the paper plate
with the cotton wool on it and the three WAITERS,
FAT, YOUNG, OLD are in line just L. of table

	and D.S. from it, passing the plate from one to another.)
WAITERS	(singing in time to music) Oh, it's hot - oh, it's hot - oh, it's hot!
	(TRUFFALDINO re-enters and crosses to the WAITERS at L. He takes the plate from the OLD WAITER and throws it with a yell into the audience. The three WAITERS go out. TRUFFALDINO spoons more foam on to another paper plate and goes off with it. FAT WAITER enters with enormous dish of cheese and begins to cross stage. TRUFFALDINO re-enters, and dashes across to him.)
TRUFFALDINO	(snatching cheese) Look out! (Rushing out.) On with the cheese!
	(YOUNG WAITER has come in with second cheese and is heading for another exit with it when TRUFFALDINO comes tearing back with another shout and takes cheese from YOUNG WAITER and goes out with it. FAT WAITER has been off and re-enters with huge dish of fruit heading for the other side. TRUFFALDINO dashes across and grabs fruit, going out with it and yet another shout, while the OLD WAITER is already entering with a second dish of fruit TRUFFALDINO re-enters, dashes across and misses the fruit. Comes back to OLD WAITER, takes the fruit and turns it sideways, so that the audience can see fruit is stuck on and goes out. All the WAITERS go, TRUFFALDINO returns and leans on table exhausted. Music fades. TRUFFALDINO stands in centre of stage and shouts off to R.)
	Everything all right, sir?
BEATRICE	(off stage) Thank you, Truffaldino.
TRUFFALDINO	(shouting off L.) Everything all right, sir?
FLORINDO	(off stage) Thank you, Truffaldino, that was delicious.

TRUFFALDINO   (to audience)   I've done it.   Served two
                    masters at the same time and neither of them
                    knows the other exists.   And now for me pudden.
                    (He goes to pudding and takes off cloth, tying it
                    round his neck like a napkin.   To pudding.)
                    What's a beautiful thing like you doing in a place
                    like this?   I am going to devour you.   But not
                    here - too many people about.   I know a nice
                    quiet place.   Come on.   (He gestures to
                    pudding to follow him and takes a few steps.
                    Pudding does not move.   TRUFFALDINO turns
                    to pudding again.)   Come on.
                    (TRUFFALDINO walks off and pudding follows
                    him.)

                    FAST CURTAIN

                    Music fades on suitable phrase after curtain
                    down.

ACT TWO

Scene One

The curtain rises on a brilliantly lit stage. It is afternoon before the inn. All the curtains are closed, and the carpet beater used by SMERALDINA in Act One is now hanging on a nail head high, just D. S. of the well at R. There is soft laughter and music coming from inside the inn at L. The table and stools are back as at the opening of Act One. SMERALDINA draws back a curtain R. and enters. She carries a fan and has one letter to FEDERIGO RASPONI tucked in her bosom and a duplicate up her pantalettes.

SMERALDINA	Here's a fine how d'ye do, if you like. My young mistress wants me to go inside that inn, and deliver this letter.
	(Laughter from inn. Music is still playing softly.)
	What? Go inside a tavern? A young girl like me? Never! And here's another thing: this letter is addressed to Federigo Rasponi. Now what do you make of that? My mistress is supposed to be in love with Silvio. Right then. What's she sending this letter to Federigo for? Makes you think, doesn't it? What's her game then? Hey, one for winter, one for summer, is that it?
	(Laughter from inn. Music still plays.)
	Anyway, I'm not going in there. Some people have to be respectable, don't they? If I shout loud enough somebody might come out.
	(Music and voices fade.)
	Ho there! Anybody there? Landlord? Waiters? Anybody?
	(Enter OLD WAITER L., napkin under chin.)
OLD WAITER	Were you calling me, miss?
SMERALDINA	Tell me, my good man, is Federigo Rasponi staying here?

OLD WAITER	Eh?
SMERALDINA	I said - is Federigo Rasponi staying here, you silly old fool?
OLD WAITER	Yes, he is, miss. He has just finished eating.
SMERALDINA	Tell him I've got a letter here for him.
OLD WAITER	Why not step inside and give it to him?
SMERALDINA	What? Go inside there! I'm a good girl, I am. You tell him I'm here.
OLD WAITER	I can't disturb him now. He's with Signor Pantalone.
SMERALDINA	My master, oh dear!
OLD WAITER	I could send his servant to you, if you like.
SMERALDINA	His servant? Ooo, you mean the one with the blue eyes and the fair hair? (Alter description as necessary.)
OLD WAITER	Yes, that's the one.
SMERALDINA	Oo - you tell him I'm here.
OLD WAITER	All right, I will. (Aside.) Fancies him, does she? She won't come inside, but she'll be seen talking to a young fellow in the street. I'll never understand these modern young girls. (He goes.)
SMERALDINA	(to audience) Hey, what if my master should see me here, what shall I say? Ah, I've got it. I came looking for you, sir, bumped into this servant, and thought he might tell me where you were. That'll do.

Scene Two

The same. TRUFFALDINO enters with napkin under his chin,
obviously having just finished eating.

TRUFFALDINO	You sent for me, Signorina?
SMERALDINA	Oh, yes. Oh, I haven't disturbed you, have I?
TRUFFALDINO	Not at all. My pleasure.
SMERALDINA	Oh, I haven't taken you away from your meal, have I?
TRUFFALDINO	Don't worry. If needs be, I can always return to it.
SMERALDINA	Oh well, I'm sorry if I've put you out.
TRUFFALDINO	Don't mention it. In fact, a little tranquil gazing in your eyes might help me to digest things a bit.
SMERALDINA	Oh, you flatterer!
TRUFFALDINO	What can I do for you, sweetheart?
SMERALDINA	(aside) Sweetheart! He doesn't waste his time, this one, does he? (To TRUFFALDINO.) My young mistress would like this letter given to Federigo Rasponi.
TRUFFALDINO	Say no more. It'll be delivered. But in the meantime, I've got a little message for you, too.
SMERALDINA	For me?
TRUFFALDINO	Yes, do you happen to know a chap that goes by the name of Truffaldino?
SMERALDINA	Truffaldino. (Aside.) But that's his name, isn't it?
TRUFFALDINO	Well?
SMERALDINA	The name does seem vaguely familiar. Tell me about him.
TRUFFALDINO	Ah, I'm glad you asked that. He's a lovely-

looking fellow. He's lively, full of spirit, a lovely talker, an extremely fine master of ceremonies, he's elegant - he's dignified.

SMERALDINA   Ah, I don't know him.

TRUFFALDINO   What do you mean, you don't know him?

SMERALDINA   No such man exists.

TRUFFALDINO   I think you're mistaken. He not only exists but -

SMERALDINA   But what?

TRUFFALDINO   He's taken a bit of a fancy to you.

SMERALDINA   Taken a fancy?

TRUFFALDINO   Fallen head over heels.

SMERALDINA   Oh, don't be ridiculous.

TRUFFALDINO   Can't you take pity on him? He loves from afar.

SMERALDINA   Does he indeed?

TRUFFALDINO   Tell me, if he was to show himself to you -

SMERALDINA   You what?

TRUFFALDINO   I mean, if you was to see him, how would you take to him?

SMERALDINA   Well, I haven't seen him yet, have I?

TRUFFALDINO   But if you saw him?

SMERALDINA   Well, if he was to my liking, then -

TRUFFALDINO   Then what?

SMERALDINA   It could be I might give him a little encouragement.

TRUFFALDINO   A little encouragement? I'll get him.

SMERALDINA   Get him?

TRUFFALDINO   He's in here.

SMERALDINA   Who is?

TRUFFALDINO   Him what loves you. Hold on. I'll send him out.

SMERALDINA   (to audience)   Oh dear! It wasn't him after all. It's some stranger.

(Music. TRUFFALDINO enters dancing, with a rose in his hand. He does the tango round SMERALDINA, offering her rose, and snatching it back.)

TRUFFALDINO   (offering rose)   For you.

(TRUFFALDINO leans over and they collapse on floor. Then he dances her about the stage. She enters into the spirit of it and follows him across. TRUFFALDINO goes off still dancing. Music fades.)

SMERALDINA   (to audience)   What was all that about?

TRUFFALDINO   (re-entering without rose)   Did you see him?

SMERALDINA   Who?

TRUFFALDINO   Him what loves you.

SMERALDINA   I only saw you.

TRUFFALDINO   Well?

SMERALDINA   You mean - ?

(TRUFFALDINO nods slowly.)

You?

TRUFFALDINO   Me.

SMERALDINA   Why didn't you say?

TRUFFALDINO   I'm shy.

SMERALDINA   Shy?

TRUFFALDINO   (nods)   Bashful.

SMERALDINA   (aside)   Hey, he's serious, he's not fooling.

TRUFFALDINO   Well?

SMERALDINA   Well what?

TRUFFALDINO   D'you have nothing to say to me?

SMERALDINA	Yes.
TRUFFALDINO	What?
SMERALDINA	I'm bashful as well.
TRUFFALDINO	Then why don't we team up? We'd make a right couple of bashfuls.
	(He starts to sing tango music and dances her to L. She breaks away R.)
SMERALDINA	That's enough.
TRUFFALDINO	Don't ring a bell? Strike a chord? Aren't you the least bit smit?
SMERALDINA	I'm not saying.
TRUFFALDINO	Tell me, purely as a matter of information, if a feller was contemplating marriage, what would a feller have to do?
SMERALDINA	Ah, now you're asking.
TRUFFALDINO	I'm putting it to you purely hypertheroretical, you understand.
SMERALDINA	Well, seeing as how I've got no father and mother such a fellow would have to speak to my master and mistress.
TRUFFALDINO	And if such a fellow did that, what would they say?
SMERALDINA	Well, if they thought such a fellow was going to make me happy, then –
TRUFFALDINO	Say no more. Give us the letter and when I come back we'll have a chat.
SMERALDINA	That'll be nice.
	(She feels in bosom and looks up horrified, then turns her back on TRUFFALDINO and feels up her skirt. TRUFFALDINO lies on floor and tries to see up her skirt as she finds the letter. She springs away with a squeal.)

TRUFFALDINO	Just a peep.
	(He gets up. SMERALDINA hands him the letter.)
	Know what's in it then, do you?
SMERALDINA	No, but I'm very curious.
TRUFFALDINO	So am I.
SMERALDINA	You're opening it?
TRUFFALDINO	Well, there might be something in that letter that would so enrage my master, he'd give me a good thump. You don't want that, do you?
SMERALDINA	Oh, no.
TRUFFALDINO	Well, then. We read it.
SMERALDINA	How will you seal it up again?
TRUFFALDINO	Leave it to me. I've got a knack that is fantastic. (He studies the letter.) Oh well, here goes. Can you read?
SMERALDINA	A bit. Can you?
TRUFFALDINO	Well, yes, just a bit. Here goes then.
SMERALDINA	Here goes.
	(TRUFFALDINO opens it, tearing part of the letter.)
	Go on, then, read it.
TRUFFALDINO	No, no, you read it.
SMERALDINA	You read it.
TRUFFALDINO	It's your mistress's handwriting, isn't it? You read it.
SMERALDINA	Truffaldino - I must confess to you - I can't read.
TRUFFALDINO	You can't read? Heugh! Neither can I.
SMERALDINA	You can't? Why did you open it then?
TRUFFALDINO	Well, I've had a few lessons.

SMERALDINA	How far did you get?
TRUFFALDINO	I almost learnt the ABC all the way up to D.
SMERALDINA	I learnt the alphabet once.
TRUFFALDINO	You did? Well, we've got the basic fundamentals. Let's get down to it. Comfy?
SMERALDINA	Yes.
TRUFFALDINO	This letter looks like an M.
SMERALDINA	Is it? No, I think it's an R.
TRUFFALDINO	Are you sure it's an R?
SMERALDINA	Yes, R's have got little squiggles on them.
TRUFFALDINO	I thought it was M's that had got the squiggles.
TRUFFALDINO	Oh well, M's or R's, let's get down to it. (He kisses her. They come up for air.) What's next?
SMERALDINA	Ah!
TRUFFALDINO	We've been through all that.

(They kiss again.)

Scene Three

The same. BEATRICE and PANTALONE enter.

PANTALONE	What are you doing down there?
SMERALDINA	Me, sir? Nothing, sir. I was looking for you, sir.
PANTALONE	Eh? What about?

SMERALDINA	Er - my mistress wants you.
BEATRICE	(to TRUFFALDINO) What's that you've got?
TRUFFALDINO	Nothing, sir. It's just a piece of paper, sir.
BEATRICE	Let me see it.
TRUFFALDINO	It's of no importance whatsoever, sir.
PANTALONE	Let me see it. Smeraldina, give me that letter.
BEATRICE	I've got it. (Taking letter from TRUFFALDINO.) This letter is addressed to me! Did you open it?
TRUFFALDINO	Me, sir? No, sir.
BEATRICE	This is the second time today!
PANTALONE	What is it, Signor?
BEATRICE	(to PANTALONE) A letter from Clarice. This rascal has opened it.
TRUFFALDINO	No, sir.
PANTALONE	(to SMERALDINA) You helped him, did you?
SMERALDINA	No, sir. Innocent, sir.
BEATRICE	(to TRUFFALDINO) So you must have opened it!
TRUFFALDINO	No, sir. Innocent, sir.
PANTALONE	(to SMERALDINA) Then you did?
SMERALDINA	Not me.
PANTALONE	Who was delivering it then?
TRUFFALDINO SMERALDINA	(together) She was. He was.
TRUFFALDINO	Yes, but Smeraldina brought it to Truffaldino.
SMERALDINA	What did you say that for? You've dropped me right in it now. Well, I've done with you!
PANTALONE	(to SMERALDINA) So you are responsible, hussy. I've a good mind to smack your -

SMERALDINA   How dare you, sir! No man has ever slapped
                    my –

PANTALONE   Answer me back, would you? I'll soon show you,
                    you witch!

SMERALDINA   Have to catch me first. Come on, then. Let's
                    see you run.   (She runs off.)

PANTALONE   Wretched girl! You'll see if I can run or not.
                    I'll get you! I'll get you!

                    (He leaves, running after SMERALDINA. They
                    chase through various openings, and leave.)

Scene Four

The same.

BEATRICE   (looking over the letter)   Poor, sad Clarice.
                    Silvio's jealousy makes her desperate. Perhaps
                    I should tell Silvio who I am.

                    (Meanwhile TRUFFALDINO tries to creep away
                    L.)

                    Hey! You! Where are you going?

TRUFFALDINO   I've got a headache.

BEATRICE   Come here! Why did you open this letter?

TRUFFALDINO   Me? I thought it was Smeraldina, sir.

BEATRICE   Smeraldina! It was you, you rogue. That's
                    twice in one day you've opened my letters. Well,
                    you've asked for a beating and now you're going
                    to get it.

                    (BEATRICE takes the carpet beater from nail on
                    wall and beats TRUFFALDINO with it. He
                    howls.)

FLORINDO   (off stage)   Who dares to beat my servant?

TRUFFALDINO   Ow! Ow! Ow!

BEATRICE   Silence, villain! I'll teach you to open my
                  letters.   (She strikes him again, throws the
                  beater on the ground, and leaves.)

Scene Five

The same. TRUFFALDINO picks up carpet beater.)

TRUFFALDINO   That's how you treat me, is it? If a servant
                  displeases, you dismiss him, you don't beat
                  him.

                  (FLORINDO enters in his shirt sleeves.)

FLORINDO   What's that you say?

TRUFFALDINO   I said if a servant displeases you dismiss him,
                  you don't - I mean, no gentleman should beat
                  another gentleman's servant. It's an affront.

FLORINDO   Yes, indeed. I have received an affront. Who
                  did it?

TRUFFALDINO   I don't know him from Adam, sir.

FLORINDO   Why did he beat you?

TRUFFALDINO   Er - he just felt like it, sir.

FLORINDO   And you didn't move?

TRUFFALDINO   No, sir.

FLORINDO   You did nothing to defend yourself?

TRUFFALDINO   No, sir.

FLORINDO   You exposed your master to an affront, an
                  insult, a dangerous situation?

TRUFFALDINO	Yes, sir.
	(Both laugh.)
FLORINDO	I see. Truffaldino, would you mind passing me that carpet beater?
TRUFFALDINO	A pleasure, sir. (He does so.)
FLORINDO	Well, you coward, you fool, you numbskull, since beating seems to be your delight, I will beat you again. Come here.
	(FLORINDO grabs TRUFFALDINO by the collar and beats him with the carpet beater. TRUFFALDINO howls. FLORINDO turns his back on TRUFFALDINO and freezes.)
TRUFFALDINO	(to audience) Oh, oh, I can truly say I'm the servant of two masters now. I've just had my wages from both of them.
	(FLORINDO turns back to TRUFFALDINO.)
FLORINDO	You deserved that beating, my good fellow. It has always been my practice to have a short sleep after my meal. (To TRUFFALDINO.) When I awake we shall go and find your Pasquale.
TRUFFALDINO	But, sir -
FLORINDO	We shall go and find him together. (He goes out, carrying carpet beater.)
TRUFFALDINO	But, sir - Go and find Pasquale together, he said. (To audience.) I'm in a right mess now. Still, best face that hurdle when I come to it. Now, there was something I had to do - concentrate, Truff. Master number one said to give his clothes an airing. If I do them both together it'll save a bit of time and I'll keep on the right side of both of them. But what with the heat and things, I'll need a bit of help. Waiter! Waiter!
	(Music.)

Scene Six

The same. TRUFFALDINO lowers clothes line. YOUNG WAITER and
BOY enter. YOUNG WAITER is chewing a chicken leg.

YOUNG WAITER	Yes? What do you want?
TRUFFALDINO	Give me a hand, will you, to put a couple of trunks out of here?
YOUNG WAITER	(to BOY) Go on, then. Do as he says.
TRUFFALDINO	What about you?
YOUNG WAITER	Me? I'm sweating. (Wipes off sweat.)
TRUFFALDINO	Oh, all right. Come along, mate, this way.

(TRUFFALDINO and BOY go out.)

YOUNG WAITER   (to audience)   Seems a good servant, don't
he? But what's he got up his sleeve, eh? In
service nothing's done for love. You get your
master to trust you, then swindle him for all
you can.

(TRUFFALDINO and BOY re-enter carrying
BEATRICE's brown trunk. They place it,
inwards, under clothes line.)

TRUFFALDINO   (as they carry it)   Careful now - over here -
that's it. Down your end. Good. Now let's
get the other. But we'll have to be very quiet
with this one as my master's asleep in there.

(TRUFFALDINO and BOY go out again.)

YOUNG WAITER   (to audience)   I don't know if you've noticed
it, but he's got two masters. I'm going to keep
an eye on him. One day he might try to rob the
pair of them. I'll report him and I might make
a penny or two.

(TRUFFALDINO and BOY re-enter with
FLORINDO's green trunk. They put this U.S.
of other trunk.)

TRUFFALDINO   That's it. Careful with it. Over here. Thanks very much, mate.

(BOY goes out. YOUNG WAITER comes to R. of TRUFFALDINO who is by FLORINDO's trunk, dusts it with his serving-cloth, and holds out his hand for a tip.)

YOUNG WAITER   Everything all right, then?

TRUFFALDINO   (shaking his hand)   Thanks very much. I'll see you at the end of the week.

YOUNG WAITER   (as he goes)   Best of luck to you, mate. While it lasts!

(The following sequence should be done at great speed.)

(TRUFFALDINO starts unpacking FLORINDO's trunk first.)

TRUFFALDINO   (taking out a book, he looks at it)   I wish I could read.   (He throws it on the ground between the two trunks. Then he takes out FLORINDO's own purple jacket, with miniature in pocket. Then a rope of clothes sewn together which he throws over L. end of clothes line. Then to BEATRICE's trunk. He takes out another rope of clothes and throws it over clothes line - just R. of the other one. Then he takes out the duplicate dress - BEATRICE wears the real one at the end of the Act. This dress has another miniature in the pocket. He holds out the dress to audience.)   I told you I'd have to watch myself with that one! (He hangs dress on clothes line just in front of BEATRICE's trunk which he has closed after taking out dress.

* Insert No.4   TRUFFALDINO then moves to FLORINDO's trunk which is still open and takes out corset and brings it to C. It is folded in half, and he lets it fall open.
Music - 'La ci darem', Don Giovanni.

As corset opens, loud concertina chord, and
TRUFFALDINO looks surprised and then plays
corset like a concertina. Soft and loud chords.
TRUFFALDINO starts to sing to the chords and
then picks up the refrain.)

(singing as a man)   You'll lay your hand in
mine, dear,
Softly you'll whisper, 'yes'.
'Tis not so far to go, dear,
Your heart is mine, confess.

(TRUFFALDINO climbs on BEATRICE's trunk so
that his head appears above the dress. He puts
corset over his head like a bonnet.)

(Singing high, like a girl.)   What answer shall
I give him?
My heart will not be still.
I long to be a lady
Surely he means no i-i-ill
Surely he means no ill.
(Gets off trunk and round to L. of dress. Singing
as man.)   Come then my fairest treasure.
(On to trunk again as girl. This time without
corset but holding skirts of dress and moving it
slightly in time to music. Singing as girl.)
Surely he'll no-ot de-ceive me
          he'll no-ot de-ceive me
          he'll no-ot de-ceive mo-e-e.
(He shakes dress which falls off line.
TRUFFALDINO clasps hands in front of crutch,
saying a soprano 'Oh!' He then clears his
throat two or three times. BRIGHELLA enters.
Music stops as dress falls.)

BRIGHELLA	Boy!
TRUFFALDINO	(in deep voice) 'Ullo!
BRIGHELLA	Will you and that soprano shut up and –
TRUFFALDINO BRIGHELLA	(together) Off you go!

	(BRIGHELLA goes out. TRUFFALDINO jumps off trunk and comes D.R. Music starts again.)
TRUFFALDINO	(singing as man) You'll lay your hand in mine, dear, Softly you'll whisper, 'yes'. (Shouts as man.) Goodbye! (Singing as girl.) 'Tis not so far to go, dear, Your heart i-i-i-is mine Co-o-o-o-on- (Sings as man.) Fe - (And jumps an octave as girl.) - ess!
	(End of music. TRUFFALDINO bows to audience as man and curtsies as girl, then picks up dress. * TRUFFALDINO comes D.S. feeling in pocket of dress.)
TRUFFALDINO	Let's have a look in the pockets. Any sugared almonds? Nobility loves its little nibble on the quiet. (Feeling in pocket and bringing out a small miniature.) What's this? A portrait! What a handsome lad! It looks rather like my master, Florindo, in there, but it can't be him. He hasn't got a moustache in this.
FLORINDO	(off, sleepily) Truffaldino!
TRUFFALDINO	Strike me! He's woken up. If he comes out here he'll want to know whose this trunk is and I'll be in a right mess then. Quick, Truff, get the things back.
FLORINDO	(off, louder) Truffaldino!
TRUFFALDINO	Coming, sir. (He starts to shove back the clothes. He appears to shove the miniature into the pocket of FLORINDO's purple jacket - there is already a duplicate set there. He puts the jacket in the trunk with other articles.) Won't be a moment, sir. I've one or two things to do and I'll be with you in a flash, sir. Struth, I've mixed them all up! (Shoving other clothes into BEATRICE's trunk.)

FLORINDO   (off, yells)   Truffaldino! Are you coming, or do I have to come out there and beat you again?

(TRUFFALDINO is frantically getting the remaining clothes into trunks. Last of all he picks up the diary, hesitates and throws it into BEATRICE's trunk and closes them both.)

TRUFFALDINO   No, sir, anything but that, sir. I'm right with you, sir.   (He appears to haul up clothes line.)

Scene Seven

The same. FLORINDO enters wearing dressing-gown. He looks at TRUFFALDINO hauling rope.

FLORINDO   What on earth are you doing?

TRUFFALDINO   Never idle, sir. I was just about to give your clothes an airing

FLORINDO   (crossing L. to table, glancing at BEATRICE's trunk)   Whose trunk is that?

TRUFFALDINO   Mystery, sir. Some guest or other staying at the inn.

FLORINDO   (taking off dressing-gown and putting it on table) I think I'll wear my other purple coat. Give it to me, please.

TRUFFALDINO   (going to FLORINDO's trunk and opening it) One purple coat, sir, coming up.   (He helps FLORINDO on with it.)   Lovely cut, sir.

(FLORINDO pats his pockets and feels something there. He takes out the miniature.)

FLORINDO	What's this?
TRUFFALDINO	(breaking C.) That's torn it.
FLORINDO	(looking at miniature, comes D.L. addressing the audience) Good heavens! This is my portrait! The very portrait I gave to my beloved Beatrice! Tell me, you, how did this portrait find its way into my jacket?
TRUFFALDINO	(aside) Oh, dear! Come on – inspiration – think! Think!
FLORINDO	Do you hear me? How did this portrait find its way into my pocket?
	(FLORINDO backs TRUFFALDINO to BEATRICE's trunk and TRUFFALDINO sits on it. FLORINDO stands L. of him menacingly.)
TRUFFALDINO	I can tell you in a flash, sir.
FLORINDO	Well, then, tell me.
TRUFFALDINO	Er – (Aside.) Got it! (He swings round on trunk to face FLORINDO.) The portrait's mine, sir.
FLORINDO	Yours?
TRUFFALDINO	(rising) Yes, sir, I popped it into your trunk for safety. Do forgive me, sir.
FLORINDO	Where did you get it?
TRUFFALDINO	It was left me.
FLORINDO	What?
TRUFFALDINO	Inherited from my previous master.
FLORINDO	Inherited?
TRUFFALDINO	Yes, sir, inherited. The master before you, sir, I served honest and well and, when he died, he left me that portrait as a token of his appreciation.
FLORINDO	Died? When did he die?

TRUFFALDINO   What's today, sir? Thursday? About a week ago today, sir.

FLORINDO   And what was the name of this master?

TRUFFALDINO   Name, sir? He didn't have a name. He was travelling incognito.

FLORINDO   Incognito? How long did you serve him?

TRUFFALDINO   Oh, about a week or ten days.

FLORINDO   (aside)   Oh heavens! I tremble at the thought that it was Beatrice. She fled in man's dress. She travelled incognito. Oh, if this be true!

TRUFFALDINO   (aside)   He seems to be soaking it up all right.

FLORINDO   Tell me, my man -

TRUFFALDINO   (aside)   Looks like he's ready for another basinful.   (To FLORINDO.)   Yes, sir?

FLORINDO   Tell me, my man, was he very young, your master?

TRUFFALDINO   Oh, a youth, sir.

FLORINDO   (aside)   'Tis she, without a doubt.   (To TRUFFALDINO.)   Tell me, what town did he come from?

TRUFFALDINO   Town, sir? I've got it right at the tip of my tongue, sir.

FLORINDO   Turin, perhaps?

TRUFFALDINO   That's it. Turin. Exactly, sir.

FLORINDO   And he's dead?

TRUFFALDINO   Oh, quite, quite dead.

FLORINDO   How did he die?

TRUFFALDINO   Er - accident, sir. He was thrown off his horse.

FLORINDO   (aside)   Oh, reckless girl!   (To

	TRUFFALDINO.) Where buried?
TRUFFALDINO	Where buried?
FLORINDO	I must visit the grave.
TRUFFALDINO	(aside) There's a difficulty! (To FLORINDO.) A fellow countryman turned up with a licence and shipped the coffin back home.
FLORINDO	And this fellow countryman - is he the same fellow who asked you to collect the letters from the post?
TRUFFALDINO	The same man, sir?
FLORINDO	Pasquale?
TRUFFALDINO	You've hit it, sir, Pasquale, precisely!
FLORINDO	(aside) Then I have no hope. She is dead. My beloved Beatrice is dead. Oh, how great is my grief! It is too much to bear! (FLORINDO goes out in despair.)

Scene Eight

The same.

TRUFFALDINO	What's up with him, then? Did you see the tears in his eyes? All upset. I did that. I didn't mean to upset him. I just told him that story so that I wouldn't get another beating. It's that portrait's fault. Some friend of his or other. Oh, how sad! How very sad! Oh, well, enough on my mind without worrying about his troubles. (He gets dressing-gown and puts it in FLORINDO's trunk.) Get this stuff out

of the way before I drop myself right in it. Hold
on, Truff lad, make sure the coast is clear.
(He hears BEATRICE's voice off-stage, and
makes a dash for the clothes line.)

(BEATRICE and PANTALONE enter with hats
and sticks, talking business.)

BEATRICE	I assure you, Signor Pantalone, some of the invoices you sent me, I have received them twice over.
PANTALONE	Duplicated eh?
BEATRICE	I'm afraid so.
PANTALONE	I shall have to look into this.
BEATRICE	Truffaldino!
TRUFFALDINO	Sir?
BEATRICE	What's my trunk doing out here?
TRUFFALDINO	You told me to give your clothes an airing, sir.
BEATRICE	Good man. You've done it, then?
TRUFFALDINO	I was just getting around to it.
BEATRICE	You idler, what do you do with your time, for heaven's sake?
TRUFFALDINO	(aside) I could tell him'
BEATRICE	Well, open my trunk and give me my - whose trunk is this? (Pointing to FLORINDO's trunk.)
TRUFFALDINO	Some guest or other staying at the inn, sir.
BEATRICE	Give me my memo book. You'll find it in there.
TRUFFALDINO	One memo book. (He opens BEATRICE's trunk.)

(BEATRICE is standing R. of PANTALONE who
is to the side of the table.)

PANTALONE	I'll have words to say to those copy-clerks of

mine. We can't have errors like this.

BEATRICE   Perhaps the mistake is on my side. Anyway we shall see.

TRUFFALDINO   Here we are, sir!

BEATRICE   Thank you.   (BEATRICE takes the book without looking at it too closely.)   What's this? This isn't mine.

TRUFFALDINO   (aside)   Here we go again!

BEATRICE   These are letters I wrote to Florindo. His diary! The hours of our meetings, our secret rendezvous. How is this?

PANTALONE   What is it, Signor? Is anything the matter?

BEATRICE   Truffaldino, how comes this book amongst my things?

TRUFFALDINO   (aside)   I'll use the same rigmarole as I tried with the other fellow. It worked with him, so why not now? The plain, unvarnished truth is this: the book is mine.

BEATRICE   Yours?

TRUFFALDINO   I popped it in your trunk for safety. Do forgive me, sir.

BEATRICE   Yours? How can it be yours? When you gave it me, you would have recognised it.

TRUFFALDINO   (aside)   This one's a bit more subtle. We're dealing with a brain here.

BEATRICE   Well?

TRUFFALDINO   I've only just acquired it, sir, no time to peruse it over as one might say. I forgot it was mine, almost.

BEATRICE   Where did you get it?

TRUFFALDINO   The gentleman I was serving here in Venice suddenly decided to pay his debt to nature.

BEATRICE	What!
TRUFFALDINO	You've hit it. He croaked it! He left me the book.
BEATRICE	How long ago was this?
TRUFFALDINO	About a week or ten days.
BEATRICE	In Venice?
TRUFFALDINO	In Venice.
BEATRICE	How comes it, then, I found you in Verona?
TRUFFALDINO	(aside) What did I tell you? Brain power! Brain power!
BEATRICE	Answer me, please.
TRUFFALDINO	I was so overcome by my poor master's defunction, I went to Verona for a change of air.
BEATRICE	Can it be true? My Florindo - no more?
TRUFFALDINO	Ah! Perchance I heard you mention the name Florindo?
BEATRICE	Well?
TRUFFALDINO	(hand to brow) Oh, how strange is life! (Aside.) Best play it by ear. (Then.) O, Fato, what blows you deal!
BEATRICE	You mean your master -
TRUFFALDINO	Yes, Florindo was his name.
BEATRICE	Aretusi?
TRUFFALDINO	Aretusi - the same.
BEATRICE	Dead?
TRUFFALDINO	Oh, quite dead.
BEATRICE	How did he die? Where is he buried?
TRUFFALDINO	You'd like to visit the grave, no doubt? Well, he fell in the Canal, he bobbed up three times and he hasn't been seen since.

BEATRICE   Dead? Florindo dead? If dead, what is life to
                  me? I leave my home, my family. I smother
                  my woman's heart in man's apparel –

                  (TRUFFALDINO mimes the words 'woman's
                  heart' to audience.)

                  I face dangers, I hazard all – for what? For
                  Florindo. And Florindo is no more. O,
                  miserable Beatrice!

                  (TRUFFALDINO mimes word 'Beatrice' to
                  audience.)

                  There is but one way, then. Florindo, I shall
                  soon be with you.   (She goes out.)

PANTALONE   (gripped with astonishment at both the speech and
                  desperation of BEATRICE)   Truffaldino!

TRUFFALDINO   Signor!

PANTALONE   A woman.

TRUFFALDINO   A female.

PANTALONE   Strange.

TRUFFALDINO   Remarkable.

PANTALONE   I'm all confusion.

TRUFFALDINO   Snap!

PANTALONE   I must go tell my daughter.   (He leaves.)

TRUFFALDINO   So, I'm not a servant of two masters, after all.
                  It's one master and one – Hey! Hey!

                  (Music. He goes out.)

                  Waiter! Waiter!

Scene Nine

The same. The BOY and the FAT WAITER enter and take off one trunk.
The two serving-wenches enter and take off the other trunk. As they do
this, the DOCTOR enters down the stairs. Music fades as DOCTOR
speaks.

DOCTOR	Ha! How I hate and despise that dog, that rascal, that scoundrel, Pantalone! The more I think of him, the more I want to eructate, crepitate, expectorate, and spew. (PANTALONE enters.)
PANTALONE	Ah, my dear, esteemed Doctor –
DOCTOR	Ha! I wonder you have the temerity to address me!
PANTALONE	I have news for you. Do you know that – ?
DOCTOR	(cutting in) You wish to tell me this marriage has taken place. Well, let me tell you this: I don't care a fig.
PANTALONE	Please let me speak.
DOCTOR	You may rot, sir! Rot!
PANTALONE	My daughter is free to marry your son.
DOCTOR	Ho! So that's it, is it? Oh, much obliged, I must say. Well, my son'll not marry anyone's cast-offs! So? The fine gentleman from Turin doesn't want her any more. Ha-ha!
PANTALONE	The gentleman from Turin is a –
DOCTOR	I don't care what he is! You saw to it your daughter was compromised by him. You left 'em alone together – et hoc sufficit.
PANTALONE	Not possible! Listen! The gentleman from Turin –
DOCTOR	I'll not listen – not a word!
PANTALONE	The truth about the gentleman from Turin –

DOCTOR   Truth? Truth? _Veritas_ from you?

PANTALONE   Will you hear me speak?

DOCTOR   The devil take you!

PANTALONE   Very well - to hell with you, then!

DOCTOR   You're a disgrace, sir. A dishonour to the town.
              A blot upon society! O, you homo flagitiosis-
              simus!   (He marches off.)

                    Scene Ten

The same.

PANTALONE   And _pons_ _asinorum_ to you! I'll bet he didn't
              think I knew that one! I tried to tell him this
              man from Turin was a woman and he just
              wouldn't listen!

              (Enter SILVIO.)

              Here comes his coxcomb of a son! More
              insolence, I suppose.

SILVIO   (aside)   Oh, Pantalone! Shall I run this sword
              through his breast? Will it give me peace?

PANTALONE   Signor Silvio, before you fly into a rage, let me
              tell you I bring you good news.

SILVIO   What news?

PANTALONE   You'll listen?

SILVIO   Speak!

PANTALONE   Ah, good! Then I'll have you know, sir, the

	wedding of my daughter to Signor Federigo will not now take place.
SILVIO	Will not?
PANTALONE	And what's more, if you are still of a mind, you can marry my daughter.
SILVIO	Marry her?
PANTALONE	You can marry at once.
SILVIO	O, sir, I am restored from death to life.
PANTALONE	Good! That's settled, then.
SILVIO	But, sir, how can I clasp her to my breast knowing that she is claimed by another man?
PANTALONE	Ah, that's just it! The man is not a man.
SILVIO	Not a man?
PANTALONE	Exactly - Federigo has become his sister.
SILVIO	His sister? I do not understand you, sir.
PANTALONE	Well, it's perfectly simple - I hope. He whom we believed to be Federigo has now revealed himself to be Beatrice, his sister.
SILVIO	Oh, I see! Dressed in man's clothing?
PANTALONE	Dressed in man's clothing.
SILVIO	Tell me, how did it happen?
PANTALONE	Let us go into the house. My daughter knows nothing as yet. With one telling of the story you will both be satisfied. It will hold you in amazement. So let us go in, take her by the hand and be agog together.

(They go out.)

Scene Eleven

A room at the inn. There is a loud noise of voices off-stage both R. and
L. Music. BEATRICE and FLORINDO, from opposite sides, come out
of their rooms, dagger in hand, in the act of committing suicide.
BEATRICE is being restrained by BRIGHELLA, and FLORINDO by the
OLD and YOUNG WAITERS from the inn. They advance on to the
stage in such a way that the two lovers do not see each other.

BRIGHELLA	(grabbing BEATRICE's hand) Stay! No!
BEATRICE	Unhand me, I say! (She pushes BRIGHELLA away.)
WAITER	(hanging on to FLORINDO) There's no excuse, sir, for taking your own life. 'Tis against the law of heaven!
FLORINDO	Away! Let me die! (He pushes the WAITERS away.)
	(Music fades.)
	Come, blade!
BEATRICE	Come, Death! Beatrice doth welcome thee!
	(Both back to the centre, determined to commit suicide. They turn, see each other, recognize each other and are transfixed in amazement. They drop their daggers.)
FLORINDO	Who do I see?
BEATRICE	Florindo?
FLORINDO	Beatrice!
	(Music.)
BEATRICE	You are alive?
FLORINDO	You breathe?
BEATRICE	O, Fate!
FLORINDO	Oh, my soul. Oh, my beloved - my Beatrice. My own.

BEATRICE	My Florindo. My own.
FLORINDO	Oh, ecstasy! Wonder and content do vie within my heart.
BEATRICE	Happiness and amazement in mine!
FLORINDO	My love!
BEATRICE	My all!
	(They embrace. Music fades.)
BRIGHELLA	(pointing to the daggers) Quick! Pick the knives up before they change their minds!
	(YOUNG WAITER picks up FLORINDO's dagger; OLD WAITER picks up BEATRICE's dagger. WAITERS and BRIGHELLA go out.)

Scene Twelve

The same.

FLORINDO	Tell me, my dearest, what brought you to such desperation?
BEATRICE	I tremble to think on it. I was told that you were dead.
FLORINDO	Who told you?
BEATRICE	My servant. And you, my dearest one, what drove you to such desperation?
FLORINDO	I, too, tremble to think on't. I was told that you were dead.
BEATRICE	Who told you?
FLORINDO	My servant.

BEATRICE	It was this diary that made me believe.
FLORINDO	My diary? But that was in my trunk. And look you, Beatrice, it was this portrait that made me conclude that -
BEATRICE	But this portrait was in my trunk.
FLORINDO	Good heavens! These rogues of servants we have - they are in league.
BEATRICE	Indeed they are! Well, my servant's forever telling me about your servant.
FLORINDO	And mine's forever telling me about yours. What game have they afoot? We must get to the bottom of this. I'll soon fix them! (Calls.) Brighella! You wait till I confront them with the truth.
	(BRIGHELLA enters.)
BRIGHELLA	At your service, sir.
FLORINDO	Brighella! Have you seen our servants?
BRIGHELLA	No, I haven't. Would you like me to go and look for 'em, sir?
FLORINDO	Yes, I would, and when you find them, both of them, bring them to us here.
BRIGHELLA	To tell you the honest truth, I've only met one of them, sir. But I'll ask the waiters. They're bound to know the other one. I'll soon fish out the pair of them for you and if I may say so, sir, with all respect, I'm mighty glad to see you've both found death to be so sweet.
BEATRICE	(shaking hands across FLORINDO with BRIGHELLA) Thank you, Brighella.
BRIGHELLA	(to BEATRICE) Ever your servant, sir - (To FLORINDO, shaking his hand.) and madam.
	(BRIGHELLA goes out. FLORINDO registers being called 'madam'.)

Scene Thirteen

The same.

FLORINDO	(urgently) Tell me, Beatrice, quickly – Federigo, your brother, is he dead?
BEATRICE	Do you doubt it? He died there and then.
FLORINDO	But I was told that he was alive, and here in Venice,
BEATRICE	I followed you, pretending to be him. There are his clothes.
FLORINDO	Why, so they are! I should have guessed. I learned from the letter that you were disguised as a man.
BEATRICE	What letter?
FLORINDO	A letter from Maria. It fell into my hands. I could not but read it.
BEATRICE	So it was you who opened it! But my servant told me he'd opened it.
FLORINDO	Ah, now my servant told me that your servant asked my servant to collect it from the post. Still, never mind. When they arrive, we must not treat them with too much severity.
BEATRICE	Not?
FLORINDO	No. It would be wiser to treat them with gentleness, kindness, and forbearance. That way we will learn everything.
BEATRICE	You are right.

Scene Fourteen

The same. Voices are heard off. BRIGHELLA, OLD WAITER and
TRUFFALDINO. TRUFFALDINO dashes in, sees BEATRICE and
FLORINDO and dashes out again.

FLORINDO	Here comes one of them now.
BEATRICE	Him! To my mind he is the greater rogue of the two.
FLORINDO	He most surely is.
	(BEATRICE crosses in a temper.)
	But calmly, now, Beatrice, calmly, calmly.
	(TRUFFALDINO, conducted by force by BRIGHELLA and OLD WAITER, enters.)
BRIGHELLA	We've found this one, sir. As soon as we've found the other one, we'll bring him to you.
FLORINDO	Yes, I'd like to deal with both together.
BRIGHELLA	(to OLD WAITER) Do you know what the other one looks like, do you?
OLD WAITER	Me? No.
BRIGHELLA	Well, go in the kitchen and find out, you silly old fool.
OLD WAITER	(as BRIGHELLA helps him on the way with a kick) All right, I'm going – I'm going –I've gone.
	(BRIGHELLA and OLD WAITER go out.)

Scene Fifteen

The same.

FLORINDO	Now, my man, while we're waiting for your friend, perhaps you'd tell us a little of how the portrait and my diary came to be changed around.
TRUFFALDINO	(quietly to FLORINDO) Sir, there's something very personal and urgent I ought to tell you. It's a matter of honour.
FLORINDO	Honour, you say?
TRUFFALDINO	Just a word on the quiet, sir. Over there, if you please, sir.

(Gestures to the right. FLORINDO moves away. TRUFFALDINO moves quickly to R. of BEATRICE.)

I've got something to say to that gentleman over there that I couldn't possibly say in front of a lady. Excuse.

(TRUFFALDINO hurries over to FLORINDO. BEATRICE walks L. and looks U.S.)

FLORINDO	Now then, a matter of honour, you say?
TRUFFALDINO	Yes, sir, my honour, as I'll explain As you probably know the servant of the lady over there is a chap called Pasquale.
FLORINDO	I should by now.
TRUFFALDINO	Well, I'd like you to know, sir, nothing's my fault. Pasquale done the lot.
FLORINDO	Pasquale?
TRUFFALDINO	Yes, it was Pasquale opened up the trunks, jumbled up the clothes, changed round the portrait and the diary. He came to me and confessed all. Pasquale, I said, you mad, heedless, reckless fool, what have you done?

He fell to his knees,   (Kneels.)   he begged
me, implored me to do something in case his
master found out, and me, sir, with my tender
heart,   (He clasps FLORINDO round chest.)
what could I do? Stop your trembling, dry your
eyes, I said, as long as you're the best friend
I've got, I'll cover up for you.   (He gets up.)

FLORINDO   Cover up? Do you know that I'm not awfully sure
                that I follow you?

TRUFFALDINO   Let you think it was me when it was him.

FLORINDO   Oh, I see. What a sensitive nature you have!

TRUFFALDINO   I was born with it, sir.

BEATRICE   (calls)   Have you two finished discussing your
                secrets yet?

FLORINDO   Beatrice, the most remarkable thing! This
                fellow has been telling me all about a servant
                whose name –

TRUFFALDINO   No – don't tell her, sir. Don't tell her. I must
                save Pasquale.

FLORINDO   You show a strange affection for this Pasquale.

TRUFFALDINO   I love him like a brother, sir. Now with your
                permission, I'm going to tell the lady every-
                thing's my fault. She can beat me, chastise me,
                ill treat me as she will, but I shall save
                Pasquale!

                (TRUFFALDINO starts backing away to join
                BEATRICE.)

FLORINDO   Good man.

TRUFFALDINO   Thank you, sir.   (He comes to R. of
                BEATRICE.)   I am by your side.

BEATRICE   A lot of man to manning, was there not?

TRUFFALDINO   The point is, I couldn't tell the gentleman, in
                front of you, what a fool he's got for a servant.

BEATRICE   Indeed?

TRUFFALDINO   Yes. A fellow called Pasquale. You see it was
Pasquale opened up the trunks, jumbled up the
clothes, changed round the portrait and the
diary - everything. He came to me and
confessed all. Pasquale, I said, you're a mad,
heedless, reckless fool, what have you done?
He fell to his knees,   (Kneels to R. of
BEATRICE.)   he begged me and implored me
to do something in case his master found out,
and me, sir, with my ten -   (He starts to
clasp BEATRICE round chest - remembers
she's a woman - and breaks off and turns round
and rises.)   I've just told the gentleman over
there that everything's my fault.

BEATRICE   Accuse yourself of a crime you did not commit?
Why?

TRUFFALDINO   For friendship, for the love I bear Pasquale.

BEATRICE   This we cannot allow.   (She starts to move
towards FLORINDO.)

TRUFFALDINO   (stopping her)   Oh no, madam, please. Don't
tell him. I must save him.

BEATRICE   Who?

TRUFFALDINO   Pasquale.

BEATRICE   You and Pasquale are a fine pair of rascals.

TRUFFALDINO   But I'm innocent.

BEATRICE   Very well, since you insist on taking the blame,
a beating you shall have.

(TRUFFALDINO breaks away R. and FLORINDO
moves to R. of BEATRICE.)

FLORINDO   No, Beatrice, no. I'm sure our servants did
nothing out of malice. In token of our own
happiness, let us forgive them.

BEATRICE   So be it. If it is your will. You are the master now. I am but the mistress.

FLORINDO

The mistress of my heart.

BEATRICE

(playing the man)   And so, sir, have I your leave to go? Presently I must join Signor Pantalone. Will you meet me there?

FLORINDO

By all means.

(They click heels to each other and BEATRICE goes out. FLORINDO looks after her and laughs.)

TRUFFALDINO

(coming to R. of FLORINDO)   Sir?

FLORINDO

Yes, what do you want?

TRUFFALDINO

I have something to confide, sir.

FLORINDO

Really, what's that?

TRUFFALDINO

I'm in love, too.

FLORINDO

You – in love?

TRUFFALDINO

With Smeraldina, the maidservant of Signor Pantalone. I was wondering if your lordship would kindly do me a favour.

FLORINDO

And what is that?

TRUFFALDINO

I was wondering if you'd speak to Signor Pantalone for me.

FLORINDO

Well now, first we must find out whether the wench wants you.

TRUFFALDINO

Ah, sir, she adores me. And I know that just a word in Signor Pantalone's ear is all that's needed. Oh, please grant it me, sir!

FLORINDO

Very well, I could deny no man the joys of love. Come.

(FLORINDO and TRUFFALDINO go out together. Music.)

Scene Sixteen

Room in PANTALONE's house. Exterior lights fade to blackout.
Stars appear. FAT WAITER brings on lamp. SMERALDINA brings on
another lamp, and stays. FAT WAITER goes out. PANTALONE,
DOCTOR, CLARICE and SILVIO enter. Music fades on dialogue.

PANTALONE   Clarice, dear, don't be difficult, please.
                   Signor Silvio here is wholly repentant. What was
                   done was done through love. Speak to her,
                   Silvio.

SILVIO   Clarice, forgive me. It was fear of losing you
                   that made me mad. I love you with all my heart.
                   Heaven wants us to be happy. Now do not
                   reject heaven's blessing.

DOCTOR   To the prayers of my son, may I add mine?

SMERALDINA   Come on, lady mistress, what are we going to
                   do? Men are always cruel, selfish, thoughtless.
                   They ill-treat us, they scold us, some of them
                   might even want to murder us. Still, man
                   wants woman, woman wants man. You're
                   bound to get married some time or other. So
                   why not screw up your face and take your
                   medicine, that's what I say.   (She looks from
                   SILVIO to CLARICE, makes a gesture of
                   frustration and turns U.S.)

SILVIO   My dear, dear Clarice, cannot one single word
                   come from those sweet lips? I know I deserve
                   your chastisement but, for pity's sake, chastise
                   me with your words, not with your silence. See,
                   I kneel at your feet. Show me some compassion,
                   please.

CLARICE   (sighs)   Oh, cruel one.

PANTALONE   Did you hear? She spoke.

DOCTOR   A good sign. Press on, lad.

SILVIO   Clarice, although you hate me for my cruelty,
                   see these tears, a token of my love.

CLARICE	Oh Silvio, you unkind creature.
PANTALONE) DOCTOR)	(together)　　You're nearly there.
SILVIO	My dearest Clarice, have mercy.
CLARICE	Ungrateful one.
SILVIO	My darling.
CLARICE	Brute.
SILVIO	My soul.
CLARICE	You cur.
SILVIO	My life, my hope, my knees, my fairest one.
CLARICE	Ah!
PANTALONE) DOCTOR) SMERALDINA)	She's giving way.
SILVIO	Sweet radiant creature.
CLARICE	Ah - AH.
SILVIO	For the love of heaven, forgive me.
CLARICE	I -
SILVIO	Ye-es.
CLARICE	I -
PANTALONE) DOCTOR) SMERALDINA)	Yes - yes.
CLARICE	I - I - I - I - I forgive you.
ALL	Bravo, etc.

Scene Seventeen

The same. BRIGHELLA enters.

BRIGHELLA	With your kind permission, ladies and gentlemen.
PANTALONE	Ah, Brighella, I have a bone to pick with you.
BRIGHELLA	You pick a bone, sir? With your teeth?
PANTALONE	(angrily) What?
BRIGHELLA	No offence, sir, no offence.
PANTALONE	Now look here, Brighella, you told me a whole pack of lies this morning. You assured me that Signor Federigo was Signor Federigo.
BRIGHELLA	So I did, sir, so I did. But who wouldn't have been taken in? What with the family resemblance and her being dressed up as a man, I made a simple mistake, that's all.
PANTALONE	A simple mistake, he says. A right rumpus you caused with your simple mistake. Oh, very well, never mind, let it pass. What brings you here?
BRIGHELLA	Signora Beatrice has arrived and would like to pay her respects.
PANTALONE	Then by all means let her enter.
BRIGHELLA	This way, my lady.
	(BEATRICE enters from top of stairs in woman's dress.)
ALL	(as she enters) Ah!

Scene Eighteen

The same.

BEATRICE	Ladies and gentlemen, I come to beg the forgiveness of you all. If this day I have caused you any pain, disturbance, or alarm, I hope all now is set to rights and that you will pardon me.
	(BEATRICE curtsies and is assisted to rise by PANTALONE.)
PANTALONE	Granted, my dear. Oh, what a transformation!
CLARICE	Oh, what radiance!
SILVIO	What courage!
PANTALONE	What bravery has been shown in one so young and fair! Don't you think so, Doctor?
DOCTOR	(kissing BEATRICE's hand) Yes, well, an excess of spirit, I'd say.
BEATRICE	But surely, Doctor, we have it on authority, love conquers all things.
DOCTOR	Ah, yes. Amor vincit omnia.
BEATRICE	Precisely.
DOCTOR	But you'd better watch your reputation. You'll never get over the tongue wagging, never.
SILVIO	Now, father, I beg you. People must live their own lives. Their business is their business.
BEATRICE	Thank you, Silvio.
SILVIO	Now that I'm happy, I want the whole world to be happy. (To CLARICE.) But marriage is best. (To all.) Marriage for everybody, that's what I say.
SMERALDINA	Due pardon, sir, but what about me then?
SILVIO	Smeraldina, now whom are you going to marry?

SMERALDINA   The very first one that comes along.

PANTALONE   Smeraldina, you don't mean it, do you?

SMERALDINA   Oh, yes, I do, sir. I agree with Signor Silvio,
                    marriage is best. But for a girl it's like this.
                    She looks around her, but she can't go on being
                    picky and choosey for ever. And if she does,
                    more fool her. She'll end up missing the boat,
                    she will. So there you are. If anybody comes
                    up to one of you ladies and gentlemen and says
                    that he wants me, don't hesitate. I'll have him.

PANTALONE   Ah, dear girl, you're all yearning for marriage,
                    aren't you?

SMERALDINA   With due modesty, sir, I'm fair busting.

PANTALONE   Is there no young fellow, then, who may have
                    approached you directly, huh?

SMERALDINA   There is one, sir. Ah, but there's a whole
                    world of difference between a bit of flirtation
                    and a ring on that finger, isn't there, sir?

PANTALONE   How forthright you are! Still, 'tis true - we
                    shall have you married, have no fear.

                    Scene Nineteen

The same. TRUFFALDINO enters.

TRUFFALDINO   Greetings, respects and heartiest salutations to
                    one and all.

BEATRICE   Where is Signor Florindo?

TRUFFALDINO   He's outside, ma'am, and if all's willing, he'd
                    like to come in and pay his respects.

                    (TRUFFALDINO moves to SMERALDINA

during the following.)

BEATRICE	Signor Pantalone, has he your leave to enter?
PANTALONE	Signor Florindo is your young gentleman, is he?
BEATRICE	We are going to be married.
PANTALONE	Oh, then by all means, show him in! I shall receive him most heartily!
TRUFFALDINO	(aside) Have you decided yet?
SMERALDINA	(aside) What about?
TRUFFALDINO	(aside) Me and you, tie the knot!
SMERALDINA	(aside) You didn't mean it?
TRUFFALDINO	(aside) Course I do!
BEATRICE	Truffaldino!
TRUFFALDINO	Ma'am?
BEATRICE	(to PANTALONE) Signor Pantalone, do please forgive this wretch of a servant I have. Truffaldino, you have been asked to show in Signor Florindo.
TRUFFALDINO	At once, ma'am. (He goes out.)
	(PANTALONE rings bell.)
SMERALDINA	(she runs excitedly to CLARICE) Lady - mistress! (To the rest.) Pardon, everybody. (To CLARICE.) Can I have a word?
CLARICE	What is it?
SMERALDINA	In your ear, madam?
CLARICE	Oh, very well.
	(They move to side of stage.)
	(Aside.) What is it?
SMERALDINA	(aside excitedly) He's just proposed.
CLARICE	(aside) Proposed?

SMERALDINA	(aside excitedly) The servant of Signora Beatrice. He wants to marry me.
CLARICE	(aside) Oh, I'm so happy for you.
SMERALDINA	(aside) I wonder, would you ask his mistress to agree to it?
CLARICE	(aside) Certainly, I'll speak to Beatrice at the first possible moment.
SMERALDINA	(relieved, breathlessly) Oh, thank you, ma'am. Thank you, my lady.

Scene Twenty

The same. FLORINDO and TRUFFALDINO enter.

FLORINDO	Ladies and gentlemen, allow me to present myself. My name is Florindo Aretusi. (To all.) I am your humble servant. (To PANTALONE.) You, sir, are the master of this house?
PANTALONE	You are most welcome, sir. I am at your command.
FLORINDO	Then permit me to dedicate my service to you.
PANTALONE	It delights me to know you, sir, and from my heart I am most pleased to learn of your happiness.
FLORINDO	Ah! You have learnt that Signora Beatrice agrees to be my wife?
PANTALONE	We congratulate you, sir.
FLORINDO	Then you will not refuse to honour us by being match-maker to our wedding.

PANTALONE	Ha! Make the engagement official, eh? Most surely. Very well, witness it. Doctor - witness it. Everybody.
	(All three WAITERS, the BOY and the two SERVING-MAIDS enter.)
	Now then, Florindo, give her your hand.
	(Music.)
FLORINDO	Signora Beatrice, here is my hand, and with it take my heart.
BEATRICE	Here is my hand. I promise to be your wife.
FLORINDO	And I to be your ever loving husband.
	(Music ends.)
ALL	Bravo! 'Tis done! Huzza! etc.
SILVIO	(to FLORINDO) I congratulate you, sir.
CLARICE	(to BEATRICE) May you be very happy.
BEATRICE	And you too, my dear.
CLARICE	(squeezing SILVIO's hand) Well, I'll always be happy with Silvio.
PANTALONE	Oh, yes! Two engagements under my roof in the one day. Who would have thought it? All is settled; all is come to rights.
TRUFFALDINO	(to FLORINDO, drawing him aside) Signor Florindo, first and foremost, many congratulations, sir.
FLORINDO	Thank you, my man.
TRUFFALDINO	You haven't forgotten your promise, sir?
FLORINDO	What promise was that?
TRUFFALDINO	Signor Pantalone - Smeraldina and myself.
FLORINDO	Ah! I remember. I'll see to it at once. Signor Pantalone, although it is the first time I have had the honour of knowing you, may I dare

                              to ask you a favour?

PANTALONE	I am at your command, sir. In any way I can, I will serve you.
FLORINDO	My servant craves as wife your maidservant. Have you any objections to the match?
SMERALDINA	(aside) Glory be! Another one wants me. Who the devil is it? I wonder what he's like.
PANTALONE	No objection whatsoever. I agree to it most happily. (To SMERALDINA.) There you are. I've done what you asked for. What do you say?
SMERALDINA	Who is it?
PANTALONE	I don't know.
SMERALDINA	Ah well, first come, first served. I only hope he turns out all right.
CLARICE	A moment! Signor Florindo, you have forestalled me in something I intended to do.
FLORINDO	Oh!
CLARICE	I had been asked to give Smeraldina to the manservant to Lady Beatrice.
FLORINDO	Oh dear!
TRUFFALDINO	Here we go!
CLARICE	Still, you spoke first, so there's no more to be said.
FLORINDO	No - no - no - no, I cannot allow it. Since you have taken this interest, dear lady, I withdraw completely from the affair.
CLARICE	In truth, sir, you are our guest, so I cannot allow my interest to take preference over yours.
FLORINDO	Ah, you are too kind. But a guest must not take such advantages. In order that you may have complete freedom in this matter, I absolutely forbid my servant to marry her.

CLARICE	Well, if your man is not to marry her, then neither must the other fellow. Fair is fair, don't you think?
TRUFFALDINO	(aside) Marvellous! Isn't it? They swop compliments and I stay wifeless.
SMERALDINA	(aside) I'll be on the shelf, that's what!
PANTALONE	Come now, let's be sensible. The girl needs a husband. So then, which is it to be?
FLORINDO	She'll not marry mine, sir. It would be an insult to Signora Clarice.
CLARICE	And I'll be no party in offending Signor Florindo.
TRUFFALDINO	(coming to C.) Sir, madam, would you allow me to settle matters? Please, Signor Florindo, did you not demand Smeraldina as wife for your servant?
FLORINDO	You've just heard me do it.
TRUFFALDINO	Signora Clarice, did you not decide Smeraldina should marry the servant of Signora Beatrice?
CLARICE	That was my intention.
TRUFFALDINO	There we are then! Smeraldina, give us your hand.
PANTALONE	What's that? Take her hand? Who the devil do you think you are to take her hand?
TRUFFALDINO	I, sir, am the servant of Signor Florindo.
ALL	What?
TRUFFALDINO	I am also the servant of Signora Beatrice.
FLORINDO	What?
TRUFFALDINO	I'm the servant of the both of you.
ALL	What?
FLORINDO	Signora Beatrice - where is your servant?
BEATRICE	Why, here! Truffaldino, of course.

FLORINDO	Truffaldino! No - no - no. Truffaldino is my servant.
BEATRICE	No, yours is Pasquale.
FLORINDO	Pasquale? No - no - no - no! Pasquale is - (He breaks off and looks at TRUFFALDINO.) Oh, I see - what have you been up to? You rogue!
BEATRICE	Cheat!
FLORINDO	Trickster!
BEATRICE	Dodger!
FLORINDO	Rascal!
BEATRICE	Knave!
FLORINDO	Tried to serve two masters at the same time, did you?
TRUFFALDINO	I plead mitigating circumstances! There was no malice aforethought. I went into it without thinking, and it didn't last long. But at least I can boast you this; you would never have found me out if I hadn't fallen in love.

(He holds out his hand to SMERALDINA who runs to his L. Then, to the audience.)

But if you can find it in your hearts to forgive me, I promise you this. Never again, as long as I live, will I ever aspire to be -

(He swings SMERALDINA to his other side - and the other two couples come down level - SILVIO and CLARICE at his R. - FLORINDO and BEATRICE at his L.)

the Servant of Two Masters.

FAST CURTAIN

PROPERTY PLOT

This covers action and business as in the London production and
therefore in this script. Alterations may be made to the business and
to the properties required in order to tailor the production to the
demands of the stage, casting, etc.

ACT ONE

Table U. L.
Stools round it

Hat   )
Stick)   (PANTALONE)

Tray (SERVANT)
  Jug of wine
  Two glasses

Hat   )
Stick   )
Gloves   )   (BEATRICE)
Four letters)
(SERVANT takes the hat, stick
and gloves O.S. and retains them
to bring back)

*Insert 1

Ice cream cart on wheels (BOY)

Straw mat   )
Carpet beater)   (SMERALDINA)

Shopping basket (SERVING GIRL)

Musical instruments (MUSICIANS)

Napkin   )
  (keeps this throughout)   ) (OLD
Duster   ) WAITER)

Hat (BRIGHELLA)

Top hat   )
Sword-stick   ) (FLORINDO)
Coins   )
Snuff box, with snuff)

Large trunk   )
Wicker basket)   (PORTER)
Carpet bag   )
Butterfly net)

Sword stick (SILVIO)

Second trunk (SECOND
              PORTER)

Three letters   )   (TRUFF.)
Bread in pocket)

Basket of bread) (YOUNG
Napkin   ) WAITER)
  (keeps this throughout)

Key (BEATRICE)

Key (FLORINDO)

Handkerchief)   (PANTALONE)
Pistol   )

Sword-stick   )   (BEATRICE)
Letter of credit)

Large tray   )
  Two place   )
  settings   ) (FAT
  Cloth for   ) WAITER)
  pudding   )
  Table cloth   )
Napkin   )
  (keeps this throughout)

Medium tray)
  Bread   ) (YOUNG
  Jug of wine) WAITER)
  Two glasses)

Small tray   )
  Silver vase   )
  Rose   )
Larger tray   )
  Four dessert plates) (OLD
  Two soup plates   ) WAITER)
  Plate grated cheese)
  Plate croutons   )
  One table spoon   )

Tureen of soup   )
Ladle   ) (TRUFF.)
Table spoon in pocket)

Covered dish of lasagne) (YOUNG
Fork in it   ) WAITER)

Covered dish of fish)
Small tray   ) (OLD
  Two fish knives   ) WAITER)
  One fish fork   )

One soup plate   ) (TRUFF.)
One breakable plate)

Duplicate soup   (YOUNG
tureen (throwable)   WAITER)

'Pea soup' (to spatter
FAT WAITER with)

Covered fricassee dish) (YOUNG
Edible peas   ) WAITER)

Dish trick
spaghetti   (OLD WAITER)

Covered dish meat
balls   (YOUNG WAITER)

Large pudding on trolley
(string with loop ready in
wings)   (FAT WAITER)

Pile of trick plates   (TRUFF.)
(breakable one on top)

Lit burner (FAT WAITER)

Frying pan   )
Cylinder and balloon) (YOUNG
Flash charges   ) WAITER)
No. 1 liquid   )

Tray   )
  No. 2 liquid in bottle) (OLD
  Spoon   ) WAITER)
  Dish dry ice   )
  Paper plates   )
  (cotton wool on top one)

Two cheese dishes (FAT WAITER
                and YOUNG
                WAITER)

Two dishes of fruit (FAT WAITER
(fruit is stuck to   and OLD
dishes)   WAITER)

In interval

Close all curtains
Hang carpet heater R.
Hang clothes line
Re-set table and stools as at
Act One opening

ACT TWO

Fan   )
Letter in bosom)
Duplicate letter) (SMERALDINA)
in pantalettes   )

Napkin under chin (OLD WAITER)

Napkin under chin (TRUFF.)

Rose

Chicken leg (YOUNG WAITER)

BEATRICE's trunk)
  Rope of clothes   ) (TRUFF.
  sewn together   ) and
  Dress - miniature) BOY)
  in pocket   )

FLORINDO's trunk
   Rope of clothes
   Diary
   Jacket - miniature
   in pocket
   Corsets

*Insert 4

Hat)
Stick) (BEATRICE)

Hat)
Stick) (PANTALONE)

Sword (SILVIO)

Dagger (BEATRICE)

Dagger (FLORINDO)

Lamp (lit) (FAT WAITER)

Lamp (lit) (SMERALDINA)

MADE AND PRINTED IN GREAT BRITAIN BY
LATIMER TREND & COMPANY LTD PLYMOUTH
MADE IN ENGLAND